the
Welcomer Edge

the Welcomer Edge

UNLOCKING *the* SECRETS
to REPEAT BUSINESS

Richard R. Shapiro

First edition: February 2012

Manufactured in the United States of America
ISBN: 978-0-9890370-0-6

Library of Congress Cataloging-in-Publication data are on file.

0   9   8   7   6   5   4   3   2   1

Cover design by Victor Mingovits

TO MY BELOVED WIFE, SHELLEY,
THE ULTIMATE WELCOMER.

CONTENTS

CHAPTER 11 | Finding Authentic
Welcomers: Let the Quest Begin

FOREWORD

....

SAYKHEL IS THE Yiddish word for "common sense." My friend Richard Shapiro's book is a treasure trove of *saykhel*. Welcome the customer with a smile. Remember the customer's name. Remember the customer's last purchase. As you read this engaging and informative journey through customer service in America, you'll find yourself saying, "of course," "obviously," "undeniable," "well, duh!" *Saykhel*.

Richard and I both learned the saykhel of customer service from working in our father's shops. My dad was a butcher; his was a haberdasher. They taught us that every customer is precious. The customer in front of us is not just about today's sale; he or she is about next week's sale, next month's sale, and next year's sale. When you build a relationship with a customer, when you provide a good product or service at a fair price, when you welcome, smile, schmooze, and deliver, the odds are that your customer will remain loyal to you and your business.

That idea became clear to me one Saturday morning in my dad's butcher shop in the farmers market in Perth Amboy, New Jersey. I was home from college, a couple of weeks before graduation, working behind the counter, when a long-time customer said to me, "I hear you're graduating college. Congratulations. You should thank me."

He saw the puzzled look on my face. Thank *him*? What about my old man, who wrote the tuition checks?

"I've been a regular customer of your father's for the past twenty years. I helped pay for your college education."

The light was switched on in my head. The customer was right.

"Thank you," I said, with a smile.

Every customer is a treasure.

And yet, most companies are clueless about that basic fact of life. Why?

The problem with customer service in America and the world is that most companies don't value—or don't know how to value—superior service. How do you measure service? As Albert Einstein once said, "Not everything that can be counted counts, and not everything that counts can be counted." The best way to count the value of customer service is to look at the bottom line. Are you making money or not?

Another reason that customer service is so lacking: most companies are set up for the benefit of the company, not the customer. Their systems and procedures are designed to make life easier for themselves; the customer just has to adjust. The great customer service companies are built to make life easier for the customer.

The Welcomer Edge reaffirms these simple ideas. Richard's book is chock full of stories of customer service, both good and bad. What comes through loud and clear, on every page, is his passion for this topic. He weighs virtually every commercial interaction through the eyes of a man who is obsessed and dedicated to great service and everything that term entails. He possesses unerring "customer service radar."

The ideas and recommendations in this book may be simple, but they are also profound. For example, as Richard points out, the welcomer sees the *person* first, then the customer. Everything else follows from that notion. Whether you run a *Fortune* 500 company or a neighborhood deli, you can use *The Welcomer Edge* as a primer for identifying (and hiring) men and women who want to give service, and as a tool for instituting and encouraging the nobility of service in your organization.

"Common sense," wrote Voltaire, the 18th Century French philosopher and writer, "is not so common." But then again, Voltaire never read *The Welcomer Edge.*

Saykhel. Pass it on.

Robert Spector
Seattle, Washington

INTRODUCTION

The Natural Born Welcomer: What I Learned in My Father's Haberdashery Store and Why Your Company Should Learn It Too

YEARS AGO, I worked at my father's store, always during the busiest weeks of the year. At the time, I was in my early teens, so usually my father placed me safely at the cash register. I loved to count the change, tabulate daily sales, and see at what point during the day we had exceeded the receipts for the same date the previous year. It was not simply a fun job. It was an education. I was stationed in a central position for observing how my father greeted customers who may have entered the store for the first time. My father had a terrific sense of humor and

Enchantment: The Art of Changing Hearts, Minds, and Actions

In Guy Kawasaki's book, *Enchantment*, Guy writes: "I define *enchantment* as the process of delighting people with a product, service, organization, or an idea. The outcome of enchantment is a voluntary and long-lasting support that is mutually beneficial."

always had a genuine smile on his face. He loved people, so
people naturally loved him back. He automatically would engage
someone who walked through the door. He would find out if
they had just moved into the neighborhood, what they did for a
living, where they may have shopped before, and what types of
merchandise they favored. Within minutes, he'd also find out
if they were shopping for themselves, friends, or relatives. If it
was either of the latter, he'd learn if the item was a request or a
surprise gift.

My dad did not discover this information by providing a
questionnaire, a survey, or a list of prepared questions. It all
came out in natural conversation, as he welcomed someone
to the store. He wasn't simply interested in customers; he was
interested in *people.* Sure, it would be great to make a sale, but
without the satisfaction of learning about the individuals (their
likes, dislikes, background, family, and so on), his job would be
simply to exchange goods for money. And that just didn't have
enough "juice" for my father. It was the welcoming aspect of
his job that he looked forward to each morning, as he flipped
the front door sign from "Store Closed" to "Store Open." Always
interested in learning new things, and equally enthusiastic about
helping people, he was what today we'd call the ideal salesperson
or customer service representative. I know some of you may be
thinking that asking so many questions may seem to border on
being "nosy." My dad did not find out "everything" on the first
encounter. But by seeing customers as people first, he almost
always turned a first time customer into a repeat patron, and
what business doesn't want to do that? It was over time that my
dad learned what made his customers tick, and his customers
got to know my dad, a person who was a real gentleman, who

genuinely appreciated and valued their business.

This is how I learned about the personal touch in salesmanship and customer service, and where I gained my first insights into how to provide both. I had no idea that I would be writing a book years later, based on my early career at the cash register. However, what I learned *then*, every business should learn *now*: Customers are *people* first and *consumers* second. If I can convince you of this fact, and you understand how to use it to your advantage, I can almost guarantee your business will improve. And to help you take steps to make practical use of this axiom, I'm going to provide you with a second insight that came to me years later. There is a particular type of staff person who draws new customers to a business and keeps them. I call this type the "welcomer." Welcomers create a relationship with a new customer that can last a lifetime. People are so *delighted* to do business with welcomers that they will have little reason to change allegiance to the company's competitors. At the

The Thank You Economy

In Gary Vaynerchuk's best-selling book, *The Thank You Economy,* he references how business owners, such as his own father, who owned a liquor store, used to know their customers personally and gave them individual attention. Vaynerchuk states that "we have entered into an entirely new business era, one in which the companies that see the biggest returns won't be the ones that can throw the most amount of money at an advertising campaign, but will be those that can prove they care about their customers more than anyone else."

same time, customers will have a powerful reason to return again and again to the welcomer, regardless of the product the welcomer sells or the service he or she provides. Welcomers are so important that a company that finds, hires, and rewards them has a distinct advantage over a business that does not. Just who are these employees and what are their characteristics? Before I answer these questions, I want to nip in the bud a potential misunderstanding that you, the reader, may have. If you are picturing a corner store in the old neighborhood, and saying to yourself, "sure that's fine if you're a small operation, but my business employs..." Stop right there! Before you complete that sentence, I want to make clear that I will be showing you just how important customer service and front-line sales people are to the health of *any* business, regardless of its size. The principles outlined in this book can be applied to the largest retail operations in the world or to the smallest boutique. They also apply to almost any interaction, from calling a contact center for information to registering a complaint or even making a purchase online.

Many of us still frequent our own neighborhoods to purchase a pastry at a local bakery, buy the newspaper at a nearby convenience store, or drop off our clothes at a dry cleaner. Nevertheless, so many of our purchases that entail speaking to a "real life" person are impersonal interactions, like speaking to a call center representative or an indifferent retail store clerk. Even if we visit the

Demonstrating Customer Appreciation

If you don't show appreciation for your customers, they won't show appreciation for you.

same store frequently out of convenience, the employees who work there are unlikely to think of us as "returning customers." A major reason why is that it's rare that the clerk who served us on a prior visit will be the same one on our next. It's more likely that we're repeat customers because the store is simply adequate for our needs or it's easily accessible on our commute from work to home.

Some consumers may tolerate the passive approach that many businesses take, and businesses may mistakenly figure that "if it ain't broke, don't fix it." But I believed it was a shame when this impersonal business approach began to take over, and I still do. A clerk or a telephone representative that welcomes you, makes you feel valued, and treats you as though he or she truly appreciates your business is often a rare occurrence in this era of humongous malls and e-commerce transactions. Why did my father understand those basic principles? What happened to the kind of service my father provided? Should we demolish the malls, deactivate our phones, shut down our computers, and go back to the neighborhood store? That is not likely. I believe strongly, however, that many businesses are fooling

You Never Get a Second Chance to Make a Good First Impression

When someone contacts your company for the first time—whether via telephone, Internet, or in person— remember just how important that first impression can be. Making that stranger feel wanted and appreciated can turn him or her into a lifetime advocate for your service or product offerings, whether he buys or not.

themselves if they think they can flourish while ignoring the importance of a sales interaction or one-to-one customer service for this simple reason: "It *is* broke." Most businesses just don't notice.

A recent article in *Consumer Reports* confirms my hypothesis that two in three consumers have walked out of a store because of poor customer service. According to the *Consumer Reports'* survey, 65 percent of the respondents were "tremendously annoyed" by rude salespeople and 64 percent said that they had left a store in the previous twelve months because of poor service. What's even more critical to understand is that, when a customer walks out of a store due to a lack of service, that organization has just killed its goal of generating repeat business. Without a consistent flow of repeat business, no company can survive in the long run.

The business community knows that Zappos was built on customer service. And Zappos's customers understand that even more clearly. In his best-selling book, *Delivering Happiness: A Path to Profits, Passion, and Purpose*, Tony Hsieh writes, "We realized that the biggest vision would be to build the Zappos brand to be about the very best customer service." Hsieh continues, "Over the years, the number one driver of our growth at Zappos has been repeat business and word-of-mouth. Our philosophy has been to take most of the money we would have spent on advertising and invest it into

The Four Classifications of Sales and Service Associates

(1) Welcomers
(2) Robots
(3) Indifferent
(4) Hostiles

customer service and the customer experience instead,]
our customers do the marketing for us through word-of-mouth.
More companies should think the way Zappos does—it's just
common sense.

Regardless of how many customers or potential customers
you have, you must understand that each one is an individual.
Whether you have thousands of customers a day or ten
customers on a weekend, the customer is still a unique person.
When he or she is engaged in a transaction, the only thing
that counts for the consumer is *his* or *her* experience. All the
computer printouts analyzing trends in sales for your company
or any others cannot convey this essential fact. The anecdotes
or stories that fill the pages of this book constitute my evidence
that you must treat every customer as if he or she were special,
valued, and appreciated.

If you are a "numbers" person and concern yourself largely
with analyzing data, consider the following: statistics are
simply a compilation of anecdotes. That's why focusing on the
individual rather than trends is what can set your business apart.

How can we re-introduce the personal touch in business?
Today, most service interactions tend to be robotic, and it's
not because of the customer. The salesperson or customer
representative frequently does not make an attempt to make a
personal connection or take interest in the prospective purchaser
as a person. Occasionally you come across someone that makes
you feel like he or she not only appreciates your business, but
is looking forward to serving you again. It's that special person
with whom consumers want to engage (although they may not
tell you). How often do you stand in line to pay for a carton of
milk at the convenience store, make a transaction at the bank,

buy a ticket at the movies, or wait for a table at the restaurant, and think, "Does the person behind the counter really care if I leave satisfied?" A large percentage of service and sales associates do not even say "Hello" or "thanks" in an honest, meaningful way. If that annoys you, you've just proven two of my points. First, you prefer personal service, so why wouldn't your customers? Second, I'm willing to bet that if you are treated robotically, you just accept it as business as usual. Is that how you want *your* company to be perceived?

Although most associates are either robotic or indifferent, some customer-service people make your day a bit more pleasant, and even put a smile on your face when you're having a bad day. Wouldn't it be nice if a salesperson actively made you feel appreciated and special, simply because you are doing business with him or her?

I have been in the service industry my entire life. I am considered one of the leading authorities in customer service and retention. Nearly twenty-five years ago, I founded The Center For Client Retention, which provides research and consulting services to Fortune 500 corporations on how to improve the customer experience. However, it was not until a few years ago that a light bulb went off in my head, and I realized that customer-service and sales associates nearly always fit into one of four specific categories: welcomers , robots, indifferent, or hostiles. You might ask, why is a classification system helpful to my business? It is advantageous because it allows any business to view its customer service and sales associates in a new manner.

Unfortunately, the percentage of welcomers as compared to the other categories of sales associates is low, which may be one reason why companies employ countless robots. Truthfully, in many instances, these organizations might as well fire them and replace them with genuine, non-human robots. At least consumers would then know that the business they are dealing with isn't hiding the fact that their employees do everything by rote, with no more individuality than widgets. The third category, the "indifferent," overtly communicate that they really don't care whether you are a customer or not. They almost never say "Hello" and certainly don't say "thank you," and may even walk away just when you need assistance. In fourth, or last, place are the downright "hostiles." When I encounter a hostile, I think (as I'm sure most of us do), "Who hired these folks?"

Owners of businesses and managers in large corporations may counter my assertion and say that they have plenty of business and foresee maintaining it. However, they must consider *why* customers still do business with them. It may have nothing to do with loyalty. Customers may not advocate for you via word-of-mouth. Rather, customers do business *in spite of* the service. I call these

Setting the Table

One of the most successful restaurateurs is Danny Meyer, founder of the Union Square Hospitality Corporation. In his book, *Setting the Table*, Meyer writes "you may think, as I once did, that I'm primarily in the business of serving food. Actually though, food is secondary to something that matters even more. In the end, what's most meaningful is creating positive, uplifting outcomes for human experiences and human relationships. Business, like life is all about how you make people feel. It's that simple, and it's that hard."

customers "survivors." The problem with survivors is that, at some point, they are going to jump ship. With the onslaught of social-media networking sites, word-of-mouth has become critically important to the reputation of any business. Social-media postings of a positive nature can dramatically move a business forward; negative social media can leave even a long-standing business in a vulnerable position. And with so many social-media postings being based on encounters with front-line associates, doesn't it just make more sense than ever to make sure your front-line associates are making each individual customer feel important, appreciated and valued?

I have written *The Welcomer Edge: Unlocking the Secrets to Repeat Business* because it frustrates me to see businesses that could be great successes struggle to turn profits because they don't understand a few basic principles about sales and customer service. My intent is to show how re-visiting the role of front-line employees (the ones that come in direct contact with customers) can make a business a better place for both its employees and consumers that frequent it.

This book identifies the four types of front-line workers that make up the customer-service and sales-associate departments of all businesses, and then explains how to identify the exceptional ones. I demonstrate why they are so important, and how you can recognize them when you meet them. I show you why welcomers have natural sales and service talents, and why they are so important to the health of a company. They are so crucial, in fact, that it is practically mandatory that organizations find them and place them in roles where they can interact with a company's most valuable assets: its customers. Why businesses should adopt this policy and how they can go about adopting it is the central theme of this book. If I can succeed in convincing you, whether you're a business owner or manager, we will all be happier.

I have decided to write this book now, despite the current spate of excellent books by such customer-service guru's as Tony Hsieh (of Zappos), Guy Kawasaki, Howard Schultz, (of Starbucks), Danny Meyer (of Union Square Hospitality Corporation), Peter Shankman (of HARO), Chip Conley, Shep Hyken, Robert Spector, Chip Bell, and Gary Vaynerchuk (of Wine Library), on the value and importance of customer service, because we seem to be experiencing a disconnect. While we understand and appreciate the significance of excellent customer service and know that providing this will increase our bottom line, as a whole, we are not delivering it. This book helps you identify the type of people any business needs to hire and nurture in order to ensure that your organization is serving your patrons in a way that makes them happy, loyal, and repeat customers who rave about your business to others.

How you can make people

Onward—How Starbucks Fought for Its Life without Losing Its Soul

In Howard Schultz's book *Onward—How Starbucks Fought for Its Life without Losing Its Soul,* Schultz writes: "Valuing personal connections at a time when so many people sit alone in front of screens: aspiring to build human relationships in an age when so many issues polarize so many; and acting ethically, even it if costs more, when corners are routinely cut – these are honorable pursuits, at the core of what we set out to be." He notes, "People come to Starbucks for coffee and human connection."

feel better about doing business with your company versus your competitor's is what this book is all about. It demonstrates just how important this ability is and that employing the welcomer as a customer-service or sales associate can dramatically increase one's chances of having a highly successful business. Furthermore, it shows how the indifferent and the hostile can make a business flounder and eventually fail. I am able to pinpoint almost immediately where a provider fits in the customer service hierarchy. Readers who apply the principles in this book will develop the same skill.

As a child, I was always highly analytical. The caption under my high-school picture reads "The Thinker." As a thinker then and now, I like to observe people and situations. Frankly, I am amazed how so many people hired to interact with customers just do not get it. My natural curiosity about people, coupled with my early experience in working behind the cash register at my father's store, gave me the opportunity to be a "behavioral researcher" of sorts. It is astonishing to me that small business owners, as well as managers of large companies, do not understand the importance of human interaction in dealing with customers. I'm talking about people who have been in business for decades. As a consumer, I am appalled by how many people at banks,

The Welcomer-Wannabee Tool Box

The tool box contains three compartments: the greet, the assist, and the leave-behind. How to use these tools and how to leverage them to your advantage are key components that can help any business.

malls, restaurants, and the like just do not seem to care about their customers, or don't understand the nature of their jobs. Yes, the job entails problem solving and completing tasks, but creating a connection with the customer is just as important, if not more so, than making just one sale. Establishing an authentic connection will be a major factor in whether I, as a customer, return, and I suspect that it's the same for most others.

The bottom line is that my informal observations as a youngster, coupled with my years of studying sales and customer service behavior and reporting my findings to national and international corporations, has reinforced my view that many companies could *double* revenues and dramatically increase profits by understanding that *people* are what make the difference.

When I've discussed *The Welcomer Edge* with friends, customers, and colleagues, I am inevitably asked which companies do a worthy job of serving their customers. What this book emphasizes is that it is not a question of "which" but a question of "whom." It is essential that companies find and recruit welcomers as sales associates and customer-service people. The problem is that there are far too few of them, and there are far too many "robots." I don't expect every company to find a welcomer for each position that involves interacting with customers. This book also demonstrates other aspects of establishing connections for those who may not be appear to think in this innate manner.

Can I transform some of my robots into welcomers? A robot can be transformed into a welcomer-wannabee. This book presents ideas and many simple suggestions regarding how to effect this transformation, but you need to turn these ideas into action. I have found that a large percentage of robots can be taught to act and think like a welcomer. With that goal in mind, I have provided readers with a tool box that they can use to increase their percentage of welcomers.

An integral part of *The Welcomer Edge* assigns all readers a job. It's easy to read a book on improving business; it's quite another to act on what you've read. What is the assignment? Learn how to categorize service and sales associates into the four categories that I have described. The goal of this assignment is not, however, to be an expert in classification. The ultimate goal is to find welcomers. If you are an employer, your assignment is to hone your welcomer radar, so that when you need to fill a customer-service position, you can determine where the candidate fits on the customer service scale. On the other hand, if you're a consumer, your job is to tell welcomers that they are special, that *you* appreciate that *they* appreciate you as a customer, because they make you feel valued.

As a businessperson who has for years made it his job to observe people and as a long-time consumer, I understand what skills are involved in developing an awareness of our surroundings and how to change them when we believe times call for such

Customer Service—New Rules for a Social-Media World

In Peter Shankman's book, *Customer Service—New Rules for a Social Media World*, Shankman writes, "Think about it. Customers appreciating employees for appreciating customers! It's like creating perpetual motion."

change. I intend to pass these skills on to you so that, when you find a welcomer, you will stop and think to yourself that you have found a true professional who deserves respect and acknowledgement.

Every business knows that it is critical to obtain repeat customers. It costs five to six times as much to bring in a new customer as it does to keep the ones you have. Readers of *The Welcomer Edge* will be given the keys to *Unlocking the Secrets to Repeat Business*, many of which I learned first working in my dad's haberdashery store decades ago.

1

You Will Either Love Me or Hate Me (It's Time to Retool "Service")

READERS OF *The Welcomer Edge* will never view a transaction, at either their own place of business or as a consumer themselves, in the same way anymore. Every time a store manager hears one of his associates greet a customer as they walk through the door, he will be thinking: What kind of first impression are they making for my business? Does the associate sound genuine and welcoming or do they sound robotic or indifferent? Will this interaction with this customer result in repeat business or a one-time customer transaction?

Although I learned how to deliver personalized customer service working in my dad's store as a teenager, being employed in customer service roles and as a researcher for consumer behaviors, it wasn't until a few years ago that I developed a formalized process for securing repeat business that would work for any business, in any industry, for any size. And when I refer to "business," I'm including museums, charitable organizations, medical offices, membership organizations, e-commerce sites, etc., not just for profit retail entities.

MAKING ME FEEL SPECIAL FROM DAY ONE

IT ALL BEGAN when I secured a one-week summer rental of a small bungalow at the New Jersey shore. Since I like to work out every day, it was important that I join a local gym within a short drive of my small and temporary vacation home. What are the things that go into selecting a place to exercise? Most people would agree it would be the equipment, cleanliness, maintenance, and location. However, the primary reason why I joined this particular facility was that a welcomer named Andy staffed the front desk. Within minutes of speaking to me, Andy made me feel at home. Even though I made it clear that I was only interested in purchasing a one-week membership, Andy made a point of treating me as though I were a lifetime member. To Andy, everyone who walked through the front door was a *person* first, a patron second. As soon as he learned my name, Andy said, "Rich, my name is Andy, I'm so glad you stopped in to inquire about our membership program." He reviewed my own particular preferences in terms of equipment and facilities. He then carefully went over the gym's schedule and policies. He didn't consider his job finished after I signed up, however. He greeted me each day I walked through the door. "Rich, how are you feeling today? What did you end up doing last night?" He inquired if there were any particular aspect of the gym I enjoyed or thought might be improved. Andy understood that his job title was not simply "desk manager." A sizable part of his job was to help me get as much out of my experience as possible. After my workout, he'd ask me how it went, and was really glad to see me the next morning. If you think about Andy's behavior, it makes sense. Those of us who find value in going to a gym do so because we want to maintain our physical and mental well-being. These are *person-related* issues. The fact that we purchase a gym membership is a means to that end. Andy implicitly understood that I and the other members were *people* first. Make sense? It should, but unfortunately, it seems we've forgotten.

The Welcomer Edge: Unlocking the Secrets to Repeat Business is based on a central premise, that welcomers are a special class of service and sales associates that can provide any company with a competitive edge. I have discovered that welcomers innately make customers feel good. They make customers feel welcomed, important, appreciated and, valued. Welcomers establish an emotional connection with your customers. They make customers want to do business with your business again. To better understand why welcomers are special and unique, it's also important to gain insight into the three other categories that I have developed, in order that that entire classification premise makes sense. Having and understanding these four categories will help all companies create a roadmap to securing repeat business.

The first category is what this book is all about, the welcomer!

WELCOMERS

THE WELCOMER OR "Doctor of First Impressions" is an associate who makes you feel important, appreciated, and valued as a customer *and* as a person; he or she makes you feel comfortable enough to make a connection, share your thoughts, and seek them out again for that personal touch and sincere concern. They also make an excellent first impression!

What are some of the characteristics of a welcomer? From my experience and research, welcomers enjoy their jobs. They are generally happy people and like other people. They are genuinely concerned and interested. They like to laugh, and they like to make you laugh. They want to engage you. They want to find out more about you, so they can better assist you. Most important, welcomers view you as a person before they see you as a customer who may contribute to the company

A Welcomer Is "Not" the Official Company Greeter

I think it is important to note that a welcomer is not the company's official "greeter." That many of the largest retailers have placed an associate near the door to say hello to everyone that walks in is a nice touch, that is not a welcomer as defined throughout this book. A welcomer, as I define it, is a person who handles your actual transaction whether you visit, call, or e-mail an inquiry to an organization. It could be a teller, a hostess at a restaurant, a coat-check associate, a salesperson at a retail store, a representative at a toll-free contact center, or a person who responds to your e-mail from an e-commerce site.

piggy bank. Throughout this book I outline the backgrounds of some of the welcomers I have met. You may not be surprised to learn that there is usually a common thread that ties them together. Most welcomers have a history of helping others. They have worked in soup kitchens, coached children in athletics, helped build a local firehouse, or offered to babysit for the neighbor's family. They do these things for the simple reason that they enjoy helping people. If you own or manage a company that employs people who are indifferent or hostile to the idea of helping people, you are not optimizing your ability to increase your revenues.

It's important to make people feel welcomed, appreciated, and valued, but why are these things lacking in most service interactions? It just might be that our society believes there's a technological solution to every problem. If you think about it (and stay away from the hype) most human problems can't be solved by technology alone. Technology can't make you feel appreciated. Technology can't make an emotional connection or understand the underlying reason for your concern. Welcomers understand this intuitively. They completely comprehend that their role is to *help* people, and customers are of course people too.

ROBOTS

UNFORTUNATELY, THE LARGEST percentage of service or sales associates do things by rote. An appropriate term for them is "robots." Who are they? They're easy to spot. The majority of retail sales clerks and telephone representatives fall into this category. They appreciate and value their jobs, but the majority do not have an understanding of what their job really is. This can be attributed to the fact they don't understand how crucial each customer is to the company. They perform their jobs with dignity and often with a smile. But it's a generic smile, as if they were in an assembly line. They primarily see each interaction as a task to complete, and they brace themselves for the next. They may say "Hello," they may even "thank you." But generally, they never connect the dots of the customer/provider relationship. To them, each customer is interchangeable with the next. They have learned to space out their work and their lunch and coffee breaks so the day goes quickly and smoothly. Many view their task as a chore. They often don't understand the concept of customer loyalty and are frequently indifferent to meeting anything but the basic needs of a consumer. In short, they have no future orientation beyond what the future holds for them.

How to Win Friends and Influence People

The concept of making people feel important and appreciated is not new. In 1937, Dale Carnegie wrote *How to Win Friends and Influence People*. The book was an overnight success, eventually selling over 15 million copies. The book's message is even more valuable today than in 1937, when customers shopped at their local neighborhood stores. Dale Carnegie had a profound understanding of human nature, an understanding that will never become obsolete, for the simple fact that human nature remains more or less the same. Carnegie believed financial success is 15 percent professional knowledge and 85 percent "the ability to express ideas, assume leadership, and arouse enthusiasm."

I'm amazed at how many "robots" do *not* say "Hello" or "thank you," and avoid eye contact to reduce the chances of getting into a longer conversation than is needed to fulfill their task. One aspect of my research in preparation for writing this book was to focus on and record the tone in which salespeople thanked customers. I also compiled data that indicated just how many providers don't thank the customer at all. They may understand that greetings and thank-yous should be mandatory, but may simply not like offering any. One bank teller told me that she was probably supposed to say thank you, but it just was not part of her make-up. She even had trouble speaking clearly and appeared to dislike saying anything at all. Monitoring a self-service checkout counter would be an appropriate position for a person who acts like a robot, because little or no interaction with customers is required.

Some managers might argue that in larger stores the stock is in the open so customers can go about the selection process unaided. But when I put my "customer hat" on while I shop, I always have in my mind the thought that it would be at least nice to be acknowledged and thanked at the check-out counter for doing business with the store. It might be the little extra that encourages me to return.

Transitioning from a Robot to a Welcomer-Wannabee

Although the majority of all service and sales providers may act robotically, a large percentage could be taught to act and think like a welcomer. Robots are sufficient for today's transactions; having welcomers will ensure a company obtains repeat business for tomorrow.

INDIFFERENT

TIME TO MOVE into the "dark side." Can there be salespeople and customer service associates that perform worse than robots? There sure can. Consider this scenario. You walk into a store where all the sales people are gathered around a counter, talking about what they did last night. The employees may be at their assigned locations, but they're not doing their assignments. They simply ignore the customer. And this phenomenon occurs in every business environment. Such workers are the "indifferent." They either don't care whether the customer is served, or worse, they see the customer as an obstacle to their own agendas— which may range from planning dinner to scheduling a vacation. I am amazed that even storeowners may fall into the indifferent category.

BEAUTIFUL POTTERY—INDIFFERENT SERVICE

HERE IS A perfect illustration of this attitude. While conducting my research, I walked into a store that sold Italian pottery. It had a beautiful display of ceramic tureens, platters, and bowls that could serve as decorative pieces as well as functional items for dining. The man at the service desk was tabulating business receipts and displaying body language that suggested he did not want to be disturbed. His intensity suggested that he was the owner. He looked up from his task, uttered a quick "Hello," and went back to his books. I commented that his wares were extremely attractive and mentioned this was my first time in the shop. To a welcomer, this would have been an excellent opportunity to develop a relationship. Instead, I was met with silence and a blank stare. This indifferent type didn't seem to care whether I was even in his store. I didn't buy anything, but I had a strong feeling that if I had, the entire transaction would have been utterly impersonal.

I LOVE ONION SOUP

Imagine that you're a restaurateur or work in a bistro that offers a specialty that happens to be your favorite food. What a perfect opportunity to gain a regular, long-term customer! Well, onion soup happens to be a favorite of mine, and I found a new restaurant that announced the item as one of its fortes. When I entered the establishment, the hostess didn't even greet me. I mentioned that I was eating alone, at which point she silently walked me to a small table, and placed the menu on it. That was it. She did an about-face, and went back to her station. So much for finding a local place to dine on one of my favorite dishes. I see little reason to patronize a business that signals to you that they are completely indifferent to your presence.

The indifferent are not only employed in retail establishments; there are many who love to take phone jobs. How many times have you called into a company's toll-free number and the person responding

> **Magic Phrases**
>
> There are certain phrases that should trigger a welcoming response. When customers say, "This is my first time in your store," "I have never used your website before," or "I'm new to the neighborhood," a welcomer will automatically engage the person and find out what brought him or her into the store or prompted the call or e-mail. This type of dialogue is critical to securing repeat business.

sounds indifferent and uncaring? How often do you say to yourself, "Why did I just spend my valuable time contacting this company?" And if a representative doesn't know an answer, how often does he or she offer to call you back after getting an answer? The answer is, "not often." Naturally, we don't see the person whom we're asking for assistance during a phone call, so there is a possibility that person is multi-tasking or eating lunch, per their supervisor's instructions or company policy, but I think usually the answer is that these people really don't care. They hate their job and their job hates them back.

OH NO! MY HAIR STYLIST IS ON VACATION

The situation just discussed may be further illustrated by an experience I had when I made an appointment to get my hair cut. The salon has a computerized scheduling system that provides access to a customer's history. I placed my call to request an appointment with the stylist who customarily cuts my hair. The receptionist heard my request, and then icily stated that Anne was on vacation. That was it. No offer to provide me with a different stylist. No inquiry whether there was another hair stylist I might accept as an alternative. The "welcomer way" would have gone something like this: "Mr. Shapiro, I'm so sorry, but Anne happens to be on vacation this week, but Grace, another hair stylist, frequently works with Anne's customers and she is available. Why don't you try her? She is really excellent, and I know Anne would be happy to learn you got your haircut at a convenient time." Too much bother? Not to a welcomer.

Welcomers enjoy helping others. After I hung up the phone, I considered how much business the salon was losing owing to such an indifferent appointment desk.

If you're an employer, and hire an indifferent type, you are literally throwing away your money. They will cost you customers and income. At least a "robot" could handle such a situation with efficiency, if not with care.

THE HOSTILE

THE "HOSTILE," THOSE who make up the final category, are rare, but when you do encounter one of these rude, nasty people, the first thing that springs to mind is, "Why is this person employed in this job?" Doesn't anyone notice this associate is doing damage to the company? After dealing with a hostile sales or service provider, you will often feel dismay and disgust for hours afterwards. Recently, I went into a museum. Due, apparently, to budget constraints, the museum had to reduce its staff. However, one essential service that a museum can't do without is the person stationed at the "will call" desk. It was obvious that the employee behind the counter disliked her job and hated the very idea of dealing with customers. She didn't *hand* you your pre-paid ticket; she practically *threw* it at you. You could see the anticipatory anxiety in the face of each customer standing in line, bracing himself to deal with this hostile person. There were, of course, many people on line with their entire families at their sides, which just accentuated the hostile environment.

––––––––––

WELCOMER, ROBOT, INDIFFERENT and hostile: those are the four basic groups. I've found that developing this classification process has been part science and part art. It would be great if every customer-service or sales associate had a nametag that instantly identified him or her by category. That way, it would be easier to seek out the welcomers. That possibility, however, is obviously a consumer pipedream.

Now that we have established that there are four basic categories of service and sales associates, doesn't it make sense that companies should find welcomers and place them at checkout counters and hostess stations at restaurants, and employ them as phone representatives? They also need to have welcomers who can respond personally and personably to a consumer's e-mail or a call to a toll-free help-line number. Welcomers know a voice mail menu is not going to put a distressed or angry consumer at ease. Having welcomers on your staff will provide you with the added benefit of having an employee who can teach *you* about customer service.

HAVE I TOLD YOU LATELY?

WELCOMERS ARE OBSERVANT and interested in what makes people tick. Consider the following interaction from my own experience. I was shopping in a supermarket in Manhattan and listening to music from my iPod as I placed my order. I took out my earphones and told the person behind the counter what I wanted, but quickly put them back on while he was preparing my order. At which time the young man said something, but I couldn't make out his words. I removed my earphones again and asked him to repeat what he had just said.

"You must have been listening to some kind of really great music to have immediately put the earpieces back on," the counter person said. We began to chat about music, and were soon on a first-name basis. William, as it turned out, was able to efficiently do his task while paying close attention to me, even though I was simply waiting.

"I really like the song," I told him. "But I don't know the title or the singer."

This raised William's curiosity to the point that he offered to put on the earphones and identify the song. Within a few seconds, he returned my iPod to me.

"The song is 'Have I Told You Lately,' and Rod Stewart is the singer," William said. I had never seen William before, but I was so impressed by the interest he took in me as a person that I looked at his nametag. The next time I ordered take-out, I not only went back to the store, I asked for William specifically. William was an authentic welcomer. He wanted to make a connection, and he did!

Unfortunately, many welcomers don't stay at their jobs for long, even if they love their work. Why? As a rule, front-line associates are among the lowest-paid workers in a company. Although employers complain about high turnover, they often don't understand that most welcomers want to

There Is Large Cost for Acquiring New Consumers

Depending on the industry, companies may allocate from 9 to 12 percent of their sales to attract new customers. Now, that's a lot of dough.

keep their jobs. Welcomers are caring, concerned, and "people" oriented. That's what makes them such great front-line people. But they're not martyrs. If they are offered an increase in salary from your competitor, there's little reason why they shouldn't take advantage of the offer. If they leave, and your competitor eventually does hire them, you're doubly unlucky. By not valuing the welcomers in your organization, you are risking the possibility that you may turn the tables on your own bottom line. I'm not going to provide a recommended pay scale for employers regarding welcomer salaries, but they should be paid adequately for their special talents and abilities. Penny-wise, but pound-foolish? Think about it.

How Much Is a Welcomer Worth?

Welcomers are good for business. Imagine that you are a family of four, and dine out twice a month, and when you do, your average bill is $80.00 a meal. That's twenty-four meals a year. If there are four restaurants in town, for variety you might consider alternating, and patronize each of them six times during the year. However, if one of the restaurants is "welcomer-oriented," you may dine there half the time, or twelve times during the year. That's six additional meals at $80.00 per meal. The restaurant grosses an additional $480.00 a year from just one family. If you factor in other families, and consider that now the restaurant has authentic customer loyalty, the numbers add up. How much is a welcomer worth? It depends on your business, of course, but I would make sure that a welcomer under my employ is treated as a professional. They are, if you will, "Doctors of First Impressions."

Time and again, it's been estimated that, on average, it costs a company five to six times as much to get a new customer as it does to keep those it currently has. What expenses are involved in this difference? Think of all the advertising and promotional dollars that it takes to attract a first-time consumer when he or she has never walked into your store or restaurant, or has never purchased anything on your online shopping website. It's equally hard—despite the hard sell—to get someone to call a toll-free number to purchase one of those cool items available only through a TV infomercial.

Let's see how to capture some new business.

Most towns have several restaurants to choose from. What makes you select one restaurant over another? Naturally, the food, service, and ambience will influence your decision. What if you went into a cafe for the first time, and the host or hostess showed true interest in you, perhaps asked you a bit about yourself and your family? Some common sense and helpful questions could be, "Are you new in town?" or "Is this the first time you've eaten here?" or "Did you have trouble parking?" These questions are important simply to gather a little information, but they are even *more* important because they help to create a connection. How would you feel if, when you're done with your meal, the staff genuinely thanked you for choosing their restaurant, and stated they were looking forward to your business in the future? Now, if you do return some time in the future, imagine that the staff not only recalled that you had eaten there before, but called you by your name? Imagine if they recalled your conversation from your previous visit, and inquired about your trip to the Grand Canyon? Never happen, you say. It does happen. That's how welcomers interact. It's simply in their nature to want to connect. Consider the impact on your dining-out behavior if you know there's a welcomer or two or three? That restaurant would be the first to come to mind the next time you ate out.

———————

THIS MAY SEEM like a natural place to end this chapter, but I have to admit I have told a lie, albeit a "white lie." That's because I wanted to leave one subcategory in my classification for last. This is the group of people I call the "welcomer-wannabees." While doing my research, I came across a number of employees who cared about customer service, who cared about helping others, but simply were not welcomers. In Chapter 5, I provide an entire list of suggestions on how service providers who might be somewhat robotic in their delivery can be taught to act and think like welcomers, even if they aren't natural welcomers. Robots need a tool kit. The tools held in the compartments of the greet, the assist, and the leave-behind will help many robotic-acting associates to see the customer as a person first.

As a businessperson who for years has had the job of observing people, and as a long time consumer, I believe I understand what skills are involved in developing an awareness of our surroundings and how to change them when we believe change is called for. I intend to pass on these skills to you. Readers that are corporate decision-makers will understand they not only should appreciate welcomers, but should be rewarding them for their talents and contributions. Sales and customer-service people may not have impressive "official" titles, but, as I've said, they deserve, at least informally, the designation "Doctors of First Impressions." Some may raise the argument that one doesn't need to read a book to understand this. But my many years of experience in the field tell me otherwise. Such a book is sorely needed.

POWER POINTS WORTH REPEATING

- Repeat business does not happen automatically; it needs to be cultivated one transaction at a time.
- Welcomers are a special class of service and sales associates that can provide any company with a competitive edge.
- Welcomers have a history of helping people; it's a common theme.
- Although a large percentage of sales and service associates act robotically, a significant number could be taught to act and think like a welcomer.
- Employing welcomers can substantially improve a company's sales and profitability; companies should make sure that welcomers receive the appreciation they deserve.

2

Welcomer Tales: Close Encounters of the Helpful Kind

DURING MY LIFE, I have been extremely blessed. I had loving and supportive parents, both of whom were excellent role models. I have a great brother, a magnificent extended family, and many good friends. Additionally, my two sons, Matthew and Michael, not only have loved me as a father, but the three of us are great friends. I have a relatively small, but successful, business, and while I might be the leader, my associates have always worked as a team, knowing that our customers were ultimately they ones we need to serve.

In addition to all of this, I had a wonderful marriage to Shelley, who unfortunately passed away a number of years ago. Shelley always made everyone feel important, valued, and appreciated, both in informal situations and in business. She was naturally interested in people. She enjoyed learning what was going on in their lives. Whenever I introduced Shelley to an acquaintance, she instantly made a connection. She would immediately say something that would encourage a fun and engaging conversation. Shelley was very aware of her surroundings—highly cognizant of what people would wear, say, and do. She was the archetypical welcomer.

While Shelley had her own successful career, she would periodically assist me at trade shows. I don't know if you have ever staffed a booth at a business show, but it is a stressful, grueling, and most often a boring experience. You are on your feet all day. It's often difficult to get a break, even to run to the bathroom. You are there to sell your wares, but most people just walk by and ignore you. If you're someone who isn't quite sure of yourself, the experience can give you an inferiority complex.

When Shelley was with me at the booth, nobody would simply walk by. Shelley would say something like, "I just love your shoes," or "Where did you get that cookie?" or "What seminar did you just attend?" People just started engaging in conversation. Shelley was not just asking these questions to get people's attention; she was sincerely interested in people and their experiences. She was curious, intrigued, and inquisitive, and therefore, as you might expect, she was engaging.

Shelley's "day" job was to sell credit card processing systems for one of the major banks, and she often had to convince merchants to switch from one processor to another. Shelley was great at it. She could walk into any store or business and immediately engage the manager or owner in a conversation. She would walk around the store, and inquire about the merchandise. It was as though every shop she entered was a classroom. Shelley loved people, and they loved her. She was an instant hit with nearly everyone she encountered. She was an all-around fun person and truly enjoyed life. These qualities are at the core of every welcomer. They are interested in you simply because you're you.

When I developed my plans to write this book, I knew I'd have to find a way to set aside enough time to conduct my research. I learned early on that my classification process was unique. I also knew I would need case studies to support the validity of my system. I needed to conduct my own due diligence to find enough welcomers to interview. And that's what I did. I took time from running my own business to make visits to small retail establishments, big chain stores at giant malls, luxury boutiques, the massive retailers, and, of course, placed calls into all kinds of contact centers and initiated many inquiries to various e-commerce sites. When I found my welcomers, I proceeded to reach out to them to see what made them tick.

MY WELCOMER IS MOVING TO FLORIDA: LET'S SEE WHAT HAPPENS ON MY NEXT VISIT TO THE MALL

RUTH WAS A salesperson at one of the larger department store chains, with a reputation for providing good service. But Ruth went beyond providing excellent customer service and definitely was a welcomer. I did not care how long I needed to wait for Ruth when I shopped at the store. Ruth was unique. Every time I saw her, she gave me a big "Hello." If she was busy with another customer, she'd say, "Richard, I will be with you shortly." And the tone in her voice indicated she was authentically concerned that I wouldn't have to wait cluelessly around her sales area. It only took Ruth fifteen seconds to make me feel welcomed. Ruth acknowledging me, giving me that quick "Hello", coupled with a really nice smile, demonstrated instantly that she was happy to see me. Yes, it often takes a mere fifteen seconds to make a person feel appreciated, valued, and important.

When Ruth was finally available to wait on me, she first wanted to know how I had been, had I gone on a recent business trip, and how were my kids doing. Were they still working at the local pizza place in town? Ruth was interested in me, and that, in turn, made me interested in how she was making out. I generally went to see Ruth with my wife Shelley. Ruth had that innate quality that is the trademark of any welcomer. Ruth always greeted Shelley with the same enthusiasm and interest. Over the years, whenever I needed any item of clothing, I would make sure to find Ruth. If she was on vacation, I would wait until she returned. If she had a day off, I would come the days she was on duty. When new merchandise came in the store that Ruth thought I might like, she would call me to see if I would be interested in looking at it when I next shopped at the store. Ruth was knowledgeable about the inventory as well—another common trait of welcomers, because, if you truly like your customers and treat them as people, you will want to provide them with information they might value. Ruth eventually decided to move to Florida to be closer to family. I knew she was looking forward to her move, and I was happy for her, but of course, I was apprehensive about what would happen the next time I went shopping at the store.

The clothing chain was known for excellent customer service, so I thought there would be a chance I would find another welcomer who could assist me the way Ruth did. No such luck. I certainly did not find any welcomers in the men's department at a store where I had been a devoted customer. So that was my *last* visit. Yes, the store known for super service had very nice people. They were professionally groomed and articulate. They were well trained and appeared knowledgeable about their stock. But I did not feel appreciated or valued. So the passion I had developed when Ruth had been there soon vanished. The connection was gone, and so was my presence as a shopper in that store.

FROM SERVER TO FAMILY IN FIVE WELCOMING SESSIONS

IF NEW YORK City does not have the densest concentration of restaurants of any city in the world, it definitely comes close. You will pass by dozens upon dozens if you take a walk in nearly any neighborhood. If they were all equally good (or equally bad for that matter), it would take forever to select one. It is especially nice when you find a restaurant that is a mere two-minute walk from your apartment (especially during miserable weather). To locate one in the neighborhood that is reasonably priced, offers good food, and has excellent service is something to value. Several years ago, Shelley and I decided to sample a nearby restaurant. No sooner had we walked through the door than we were greeted by Mohammad. While I couldn't quite describe it at the time, I understand now that he was a welcomer. He was extremely personable, an excellent and efficient waiter, and seemed genuinely happy to be waiting on us. He had never set eyes on us before, but made us feel right at home.

A week later, we returned to the restaurant hoping that Mohammad would be working that day. It was as though Mohammad had heard us walking down the street. "Mr. and Mrs. Shapiro, I'm so glad to see you," he said. "I will make sure the manager puts you in my section."

We had only dined there one time, but Mohammad made us feel like we were family. He even had remembered our names. I have found that, as a rule, welcomers have an excellent memory for names and faces. When we sat down to order, Mohammad knew what we ordered the previous week, and what our wine preferences were. It was not simply a matter of recalling we liked Cabernet or Merlot. He even recalled which Cabernet. Mohammad was truly amazing. There were over fifteen restaurants in the vicinity, but we continued to make Mohammad's place our restaurant of choice. That first New Year's Eve, we decided that we wanted to celebrate midnight at our favorite restaurant. Mohammad not only had our table entirely prepared when we walked in, he sat at our table for several minutes. When the clock struck midnight, we all hugged each other as though we were life-long family members. A true welcomer creates a bond that seems almost mystical. The presence of a welcomer on the staff causes you to be drawn back to the store, the restaurant, the barber shop, or even the gas station when you have your choice of dozens. But, to think about it, there's nothing mystical at all going on. What is there about human nature that draws us to make a selection where there are suitable alternatives? It's the deeply rooted knowledge that you are encountering someone who appreciates you as a person. If that bond is there, the customer interaction flows naturally.

GOOD SERVICE IS MORE THAN SKIN DEEP

....

A FEW TIMES a year I go to Dr. Campbell, my dermatologist. Every time I see Dr. Campbell, she gives me the biggest smile; she really wants to know how I am doing and recalls everything I mentioned on previous visits. She is that way with everyone, as is evident when I hear her upbeat, friendly, and compassionate voice while she is interacting with other patients. My customer-service radar is on full power when I see her, so naturally I decided to find out what made her a welcomer.

At first, she had a hard time articulating it. After all, it came naturally to her so she didn't really analyze this element of her personality. Then she recalled how, when she was a little girl of nine or ten, she considered herself the "mayor" of the street where her parents lived. She would visit the neighbors, many of whom were elderly, simply to help them out. They didn't request her assistance. It was just something she felt was a good thing to do. She would help take out their garbage, or pick up their newspaper on the porch and hand it to them. For a blind neighbor, she would invite herself into her living room and read books to her. One time, as she was reading, she noticed the woman was wearing a watch with Braille symbols. She was very intrigued by it. She asked permission to run her hands over the raised Braille marks to feel them. Dr. Campbell was always interested in people and loved to learn about new things.

It was also clear that, from early childhood, Dr. Campbell liked to help people. She was very outgoing. When I asked why she was so naturally engaging with her patients, she told me she loved to be helpful and had a natural curiosity. These traits always compelled her to inquire about people whom she met. She also loves to share what she learns, making her an enthusiastic welcomer.

When I know that I'm going to visit Dr. Campbell's office, I look forward to it. I can't wait to tell her what's going on in my life, because I just know she wants to know, whether it's about how I'm feeling in general, how my sons are doing, or what's new in my business.

HELP! I CAN'T FIND MY PAPERS

MICHELE WORKS AT my local bank. Every time I ask Michele to do something for me, it's never an intrusion.

"Mr. Shapiro, I am so happy to see you! How may I help you?" That's her typical greeting when I'm at her branch. When I ask her to print out a statement that I need for my accountant (even when I've asked her previously, because I misplaced the first one), she continually has a helpful attitude. I always look forward to calling her, even when I may be stressed out or need something in a hurry.

WILL THE REAL RICH SHAPIRO PLEASE STAND UP?

ONE DAY, WHILE I was driving my car, a stone flew up and cracked my windshield, so I ended up taking it to a glass-replacement garage. The front desk person told me to see Rich on the second floor, who was handling the paperwork. After I climbed the stairs, I saw a fellow behind the desk who gave me a huge "Hello," and cheerfully asked me how I was doing. I said

"Well, not too good, I need to have my windshield replaced, but I guess I'm in the right place." I told him that, by coincidence, my name was "Rich" too. When I gave my full name, Rich Shapiro, his eyes widened, and a big smile crossed his face.

"Well, meet another Rich Shapiro. We have the same exact name!" Imagine meeting someone who, not only has the same name as you, but is a welcomer to boot! I found out Rich used to sell comic books when he was ten years old at a flea market in Southern New Jersey, and he told me that's where he learned the value of engaging people in selling his goods. Rich understood at age ten what most service providers don't get at age twenty, thirty, or forty, and often not at all.

IT'S THE SMILE FIRST, WHAT YOU SAY IS SECOND

JAVIER IS A welcomer. I would eventually learn that he would make a positive difference in my life. He was working at my local luncheonette, where I'd often stop for a quick bite to eat. Javier was eighteen at the time, had recently graduated high school, and had come to the United States at the age of fifteen, not knowing a word of English. Javier's English was still not very good, and his speech required attentive listening to understand and was difficult to discern. But his smile was so uplifting that whenever he greeted me I looked forward to speaking with him. Javier's smile greeted me first. I could tell that he was a welcomer before he ever uttered one word to me. I knew he loved people, and that he was eager to take my order, and appreciated that I was a regular customer. He was happy to help *all* of the customers. He had an incredible memory (as I mentioned before, a typical trait of true welcomers) and would recall what you had ordered the last time you were in the shop. He would even remind you that the restaurant had a particular salad dressing or type of bread you had requested before. After we had been served by Javier a few times, he took out photographs of his family, and remarked how proud he was of his sister when she was honored for her high level of scholastic achievement at her middle school. He showed me pictures of his parents and of a young sibling who had recently arrived in New Jersey. When Javier got a new car, he rushed over to me during his break to point it out to me on the street. Javier made me feel as though he appreciated me on a personal level, as he did with the other patrons. Like other welcomers, he possessed a personality trait that is simply a part of every welcomer's makeup: he was genuinely interested in people.

I ended up hiring Javier one year later for my business. Two years later, I promoted him, and he has become a valuable member of our corporate team. And, Javier is a welcomer. Welcomers always make great associates (or, as many businesspeople call them, "employees"). I never thought it was appropriate to ask about Javier's background until I was

Common Traits of a Welcomer

Welcomers love to help people. Welcomers have a history of volunteering at a young age: working in soup kitchens along with their parents, coaching sports, and tutoring other family members and friends. Welcomers also have great memories. They are interested in learning about their customers to find out more about them. They see customers as people first, so it just makes sense they would want to learn more.

researching this book. Once again, I found a common theme that seems to run in a welcomer's development: volunteering to help others at an early age.

Javier grew up in a small Mexican town. It was part of a farming community and, during harvest time, all of the families helped the local farmers. Even though most of the families had very modest incomes, they would prepare and serve food for those that were even less fortunate. Helping had become part of Javier's nature. Caring for the less fortunate came to him naturally. Was this because he had been taught or trained to behave that way? No. He had an intuitive understanding that adding a bit of happiness to people you meet along life's journey was a reward unto itself. During our interview, he made a simple statement that summed up this philosophy.

"You know, Richard," he told me, "when I worked at the deli counter, my job wasn't just to slice cold cuts and cheese. It was to put a smile on someone's heart." Now *those* are the words of a true welcomer.

I NEED TO CALL THE CABLE COMPANY; I HOPE I GET A WELCOMER

WHEN YOU'RE FACE to face with a welcomer, you can often tell immediately, because of his or her smile, body language, or attentiveness. You can also determine whether you're interacting with a welcomer on the phone. It's evident from what he says, how he says it, and how he first engages you in conversation. When those elements come together, you know you've struck gold. Lance was one such welcomer.

The story of my interaction with Lance, a natural welcomer,

began when I contacted my cable-service provider to inquire about adding an additional cable box for a new TV I had just purchased. Lance was the customer-service associate who took my call, and he was so wonderful. I know that frequently many cable companies get a bad rap for having poor service. I think one of the biggest issues with contact centers is that the associates on the phone do tend to sound robotic. I believe that many of the policies and training programs that cable service providers obtain fall into the area of "selling upgrades" to existing customers. And, therefore, if you have robotic-acting representative coupled with a robotic script, it can result in additional frustrations.

As it turns out, Lance was not the typical associate you get when you call a company for information. Rather, he was a welcomer, and made me happy that I called. He provided me with helpful, accurate information, and quickly understood, by listening to me, what I wanted. He recognized that, by helping me, he was helping his company.

In speaking with Lance, I discovered he had a history of helping others. Lance's father, Chuck, had been a Major League baseball player, but unfortunately developed a condition that forced him to end his athletic career early. Many former professional athletes enter the corporate world, but Lance's father spent most of his free time coaching kids on how to improve their skills as ball players. Lance was the most talented player on his little league team, but starting at the age of ten, he happily assisted his dad with the coaching. Once again, we have a case of a welcomer with a background of helping others.

FAY'S HOTEL

IT SHOULD SEEM obvious that the hospitality industry would go out of its way to find welcomers, but this isn't necessarily the case. Many years ago, on a trip to Texas, I met Fay. The Dallas hotel where Fay worked was definitely lucky to have her as a front-desk employee. On each return visit to Dallas, I'd check into that same hotel, and Fay was always happy to see me—even when there had been a four-month gap in my visits. I couldn't help but smile when I saw Fay at the check-in counter. I even began to refer to the hotel as "Fay's Hotel." I could have easily selected some of the newer hotels in the area, but Fay's presence was the "glue" that created my loyalty. In my interview with Fay, she revealed that, early in life, she observed how front-line representatives could make a big difference in a patron's immediate and long-term relationship with an establishment. Her father, an accountant, frequented a gym daily, and Fay would

Fay's Tips to Sound/ Look Welcoming

- Never slouch or use cell phones if someone is near or at the front desk.
- Always remember your job is to help the guests, whether they are checking in, asking a question, or checking out.
- A customer may have had a stressful trip, and it's important to be attentive to his or her state of mind.
- Communicate to the guests that their business is appreciated, so that when they check out, they have a positive feeling about their stay.

accompany him. She vividly recalled how the gym staff made her father smile. They called him the "champ" because he spent a short time as a professional boxer before switching careers. He hadn't revealed that fact to them, but they found out, simply because they wanted him to have a rewarding time at the gym, and to do that meant learning a bit about him. Recently, Fay was promoted to front desk manager, and one of her duties is to train the staff.

A PENNY FROM YOUR POCKET CAN GIVE SOMEONE A START

WHILE VISITING SOME business friends in Philadelphia, I came across a welcomer that had one of the toughest "sales" jobs anyone could have. She was soliciting money for the homeless. She told me her name was Dawn Dusk. The way Dawn staffed her card table made it impossible to ignore her. She had a lilt to her voice that made it seem that she was singing her requests for donations. In a beautiful melodic tone, she'd repeat the following chant:

> *A penny from your pocket,*
> *A penny from your heart,*
> *A penny for the homeless,*
> *Will give someone a start.*

You could not walk by without donating the change in your pocket. And if you didn't have any cash, you'd walk by guiltily. Dawn told me she had been homeless herself for many years, and had just recently gotten her life back together. There was a welcomer, selflessly collecting money for charity on the streets of a city. I couldn't help but think that any business with a customer service department would hire her in a minute.

THE WRITTEN WELCOMERS

THE ONLINE EDITION of the *Wall Street Journal* published an article, "Customer Service as a Growth Engine." The article stressed the view that customer service can clearly give a business a competitive advantage. Companies understand this and are finally investing in customer service. I decided to add a "comment," but what I typed was simply deleted. I noticed a "contact us" feature on the page, so I entered my name and e-mail address and expressed my frustration at unsuccessfully recording my comment. Two hours later, I got an e-mail back from Demetria, apparently one of their online associates. I could discern that Demetria was a welcomer from the way she composed her *e-mail!*

How did I know? Her e-mail was written in a way that made me feel welcomed and appreciated. Her message began with a statement apologizing because I had a problem. She had addressed the e-mail to "Mr. Shapiro." She informed me that other customers had similar problems. This identified the cause of the "problem" as coming from the newspaper side, not from mine. She wrote that my comment was important to the *Wall Street Journal* and that I should call her anytime if I needed her to walk me through the website features. To sum up, she made me feel my input was important and my business was appreciated.

I decided to contact her the next morning, and I did. When Demetria answered, she gave me a big "Hello", apologized once again for the problem, and spent ten minutes working with me until my comment was properly recorded. Then she thanked me for my patience and understanding. Demetria was a welcomer. To demonstrate just how powerful the "welcomer effect" can be, consider that I recognized her type from her e-mail. In Chapter 8, I discuss how to make a customer feel appreciated and valued via Web and e-mail communications, and even visiting online shopping sites.

Welcomers can make a significant difference in how an organization functions. Having welcomers as front-line associates, that is, as cashiers, counter clerks, gas station attendants, or restaurant hosts or hostesses can significantly increase the revenue of a company. They also leave a company less vulnerable to competition, especially when a similar business opens up in the neighborhood or local mall or the customer finds a new online site offering similar merchandise.

Everyone wants to earn more money and get promotions, but welcomers do not make your customers feel welcomed, appreciated, and important for the money. They do it because they understand how to service customers. However, if your business is lucky enough to have welcomers, *make sure* that you let them know that you appreciate their commitment to service delivery. Don't promote them to a back-order job. Recognize that investing in a welcomer via pay grade, bonuses, working conditions, and so on, is a great investment for your business.

POWER POINTS WORTH REPEATING

- Providing good customer service doesn't always generate repeat business; it's building that emotional connection that becomes the loyalty glue.
- You can make a customer feel welcomed, important, and appreciated in fifteen seconds.
- A welcomer will invite the customer back; that's great for repeat business.
- Welcomers like to learn new things; they love to share knowledge that will help everyone.
- Welcomers have a history of helping people; even at a young age, welcomers have coached, helped the less fortunate, liked to assist their siblings with homework, and so on.

3

What Are Companies Thinking—Or Are They?

DID EMPLOYERS EVER hear the expression, "It's absolutely crucial to make a good first impression?" I think not! If restaurant owners, mall operators, contact-center managers, and small retailers have ever asked themselves whether an employee or prospective employee would make a good impression, I think they would think twice before putting most people in front-line positions. But this is simply the beginning. In addition, employers should be asking themselves considerably more. For example, they should consider, does this person like to help others? Is she truly interested in people? Is he enthusiastic about learning new things? Is she outgoing? Is he friendly? Does she want to engage with first-time customers or would she rather be reading a book, going to a movie, filling in stock, or doing back office type work? There is nothing wrong with the last activity, but if that is the case, don't put that person in a front-line position. All these questions point to one thing. When seeking out a sales or customer-service person, look for a welcomer. Your business will incrementally increase in revenues and profits. It's not magic, and it's not science. It's just common sense.

As I have mentioned, consumer interactions with a company are often limited or even a one-time only encounter. For example, if the storeowner or call-center manager does not employ a welcomer, it limits his chances of ever getting that customer back or calling the company to order a second product. Businesses lose millions and millions of dollars each day because they don't understand how important it is to make a good first impression. They don't understand that, without one, they may not get a second chance. That positive initial impression can result in acquiring a lifetime customer *and* advocate for your company. I am continually amazed at how I can walk into a restaurant (with or without a reservation) where the host or hostess makes me feel as though he or she couldn't care less if I dine there again. This can occur in even subtler ways. For example, a salesperson may fail to realize that, because I enter his establishment for a last minute gift purchase, I may be in hurry because of my deadline, not because I don't value the store. Does it occur to many clerks or even managers that I may have found their store by chance, but a welcoming attitude may bring me back as a regular customer?

CAN YOU HELP ME?

THE OTHER DAY I called my bank's toll-free number, and as soon as the person answered the phone, I could tell I had an "indifferent." She immediately told me that I had contacted

the wrong department, and her tone of voice indicated that
as far as she was concerned, I had interrupted her day. I had
contacted the personal banking department rather than the
business department. Consider that she didn't even have the
courtesy to explain this. Being told that you've reached the
"wrong department" is not particularly helpful to a customer.
Moreover, it is downright rude. How difficult would it have been
to simply explain this to me, and switch me to the appropriate
agent, or at least explain how I could do so myself? How hard
would it have been to show concern that I was a bank customer
in need of assistance? That *one* experience left me with a negative
impression. This provides a good illustration of why front-
line people are so important to a business. Am I being overly
sensitive? I doubt it, unless you think that common courtesy is
not an integral part of the customer-business relationship.

Unfortunately, non-welcomers don't have a holistic view
of a customer. To them, the customer is simply a one-time
caller. They don't have the insight of the welcomer, who
understands that I may have a long, ongoing relationship with
the business. The welcomer understands that I may have a
one-time interaction with him or her, but that is simply one
communication in a relationship that began long before I
made that call, and will continue long after (unless, that is, the
customer service representative is so indifferent or rude that I
simply decide to change banks altogether!) It happens that the
bank I had contacted was the one that handles the operating
account for my business. The original salesperson in this bank's
commercial department fought hard to get my business by
convincing me they would provide better service than the bank
I had previously been with. At the least, this transaction was

ironic. At the worst, it could have given me the impetus to return to my former bank.

The aforementioned experience falls under the subcategory of a customer-service interaction that I informally call the "transfer."

One of the leading premium credit card companies does that extremely well. This company understands that it takes a great deal of investment in advertising, promotion, and personnel to get just one new customer, and it only takes one negative interaction to make a customer start looking for another place with which to do business.

The Warm Transfer

In this age of computerized call responses and voice-mail menus, the simple process of being transferred to the appropriate person can be an ordeal. Let's talk a bit about how transfers should be handled. Every transfer should be a "warm" transfer, that is, a transfer that makes the customer feel like the business cares. The representative that transfers you should stay on the line until the appropriate person answers. Then, he or she should serve as a welcomer: a welcomer who introduces one party (the caller) to the other (the representative). Is that so difficult? An appropriate way to do this might be as follows:

> WELCOMER: *Mr. Jones is on the line, and he has a question that would best be answered by your division. Let me tell you a bit about his inquiry.*
> TO THE CALLER: *Mr. Jones, I have Jessica or (Jason) on the line. She (or he) will be happy to assist you.*

By now, it should be clear that I am conveying two primary messages in this chapter. First, face-to-face first impressions are critically important to the success of any business, whether it be a supermarket, computer repair lab, apparel store, discount department store, or coffee bar. If a store or contact center has a welcomer, the chances of a customer conducting return business will be greatly enhanced. A welcomer will engage a customer to discover what he or she is looking for. There is always the chance that the customer is looking for a product that has not been placed on display, but will be available in a day or two. A welcomer may also direct a customer to a location that has the item in stock. You might think at this point, "But most people don't have the time or inclination to pay a return visit within a couple of days to buy the item," or "It's not very likely a customer will drive three miles down the road on a weekend to buy just one item." That may or may be not be true. However, if that's your response, you're not thinking like a welcomer! Yes, a welcomer provides this information to assist the consumer during that particular interaction. *More* significant, however, is that, by engaging the customer so that he or she feels appreciated, the consumer has a greater likelihood of recalling the store representative *and* the particular store. The result may be that the customer drops by the store another time because he or she has a positive association with your place of business, because of the welcomer.

If you were to add up all the business that a specific store branch or customer call-center loses because the staff lacks the "vision" to make potential customers feel like *people first,* the amount would be staggering. In Chapter 9, I'm going to provide some suggestions for store owners, contact-center managers, and anyone else who hires, oversees, or monitors front-line employees about how they can calculate the actual loss. Or, conversely, how to determine the dollar value of a welcomer.

The second message I want to impart here is how to avoid the all too common occurrence of a loyal customer becoming so turned off by a single incident that he or she ends your business relationship.

CAN SOMEONE POSSIBLY BE MORE OBNOXIOUS?

RECENTLY, I TOOK a client out for drinks. The hotel we visited is part of a much larger hotel corporation, and happened to be conveniently located. When we were about halfway through our drinks, my client needed to use the restroom. I took the opportunity to make a quick call home, so I went outside to make my call to avoid the bar's loud ambient noise.

My client and I returned to the table at the same time only to discover that our drinks had been removed by the waitress. Now, maybe we could have left a suit jacket or a paper to indicate that we were only gone temporarily. However, the drinks at this hotel are very pricey, and it's the type of establishment where patrons often confer for hours. One would think common courtesy (and common sense) would suggest to any waitperson that he or she should be certain a party has left for the evening before clearing the area—not simply assuming as much. Evidently, our waitress lacked both of these attributes, for when we told her we were not finished with the drinks and that she had mistakenly taken them away, her response was less than apologetic. In fact, it was downright rude. She claimed in a holier-than-thou attitude that the entire misunderstanding was *our* fault, and in a condescending tone, told us that if we wanted to "finish" our drinks, we'd have to pay for the ones she had bussed. If she had explained in a reasonable tone of voice that she did not have the authority to provide us with "free" replacements, but that she would speak with the manager to see if the bar could make an exception, things would have been easily resolved. I would have chalked up the situation to human error. But certainly, it was her attitude that made us never want to come back. And, as I said, I was with a client, which made the experience even more upsetting. There is a way to communicate customer appreciation and loyalty, even if the outcome is not what the customer might want. It was the last time I selected that bar for a meeting with a client.

NOT TOO NEIGHBORLY AT THE NEIGHBORHOOD STORE

THE OTHER DAY I needed flowers for my office. Generally, I purchase them from a florist a few towns away. However, since time was short, I decided to drive down to the business section where my company is located in search of a flower shop. To my delight, I found a florist in a small strip mall, and since there was plenty of available parking, I pulled into the mall, parked, and walked into the store. At that point, my good fortune ended. The first thing I noticed was that the woman behind the desk failed to say "Hello", or anything else. She was busy opening packages and cutting some flowers. I eventually purchased some flowers, but getting her to assist me was like pulling teeth. If I had not needed the flowers for clients that I expected at my office within a half hour, I never would have purchased anything from her. It would have been great to find a local florist that appreciated and valued my business, since I purchase flowers for numerous occasions, and a florist in my area would save me forty minutes of driving each time I did so. So, how much business did this store lose because of an indifferent retailer? I spend at least $300.00 a year on floral arrangements for business and personal reasons. Over a five-year period, this store could have received an extra $1,500.00 in business.

I WILL SEAT YOU WHEN I'M GOOD AND READY

RECENTLY, I WAS joining a couple—long-time friends of mine—for dinner, so we decided to meet at a local restaurant at six o'clock. I arrived around 5:45 p.m., and waited outside for my friends. Well, Janis, the wife of the couple, showed up around 6:05 p.m. and said that her husband Jay was on the way. We entered, and told the hostess we'd be a party of three, with the third member expected shortly. The hostess asked us just how long it would take for the additional person to arrive. We told her that it would be about ten minutes. Suddenly, the demeanor of the waitress changed so radically that I could tell she was about to say something hostile. And she did.

"I can't seat you until everyone is here," she said indignantly. I thought to myself, "What if we had said five minutes?" Then she suggested we wait at the bar. Her attitude left us with such a bad taste (no pun intended), I will never go back. Up until this run-in, I used to dine there about once a month and bring at least one other person. If the average bill was $50.00, that's $600.00 of lost revenue a year. Over five years, that's $3,000.00. Why don't store owners and managers get that they are dealing with people first, and customers second? If they're not considerate with the former, they shouldn't expect any business from the latter. And, not to my surprise, about a month after this occurrence there were flyers on all of the cars in our corporate parking area advertising this same restaurant. The first thing that came to my mind was that these flyers were probably the direct result of the restaurant losing other customers beside me. The problem is that so many businesses don't get the connection between having non-welcomers and repeat business.

THE HANDOFF

ON A BEAUTIFUL Saturday in a former neighborhood of mine, I stopped into a store that sells healthful-style smoothies. The man who took the order was pleasant enough—a robot, perhaps, but at least he wasn't indifferent or hostile. However, the employee who prepared the order and handed it to me, said nothing; no thank you, no have a nice day, nothing. Did I ever go back? Not yet, and frankly I have no reason to give that shop my repeat business. What kind of first impression did that place make? A bad one. But they won't have a chance to make *any* impression on me again.

Each Customer Encounter

Businesses need to realize that each encounter with a customer is a critical part of the customer loyalty process. The handoff from sales to check-out needs to be conducted in a welcoming manner, in which the customer feels important and appreciated at every customer touch point.

DOES THIS PLACE HIRE ONLY THE INDIFFERENT ON PURPOSE?

I HAVE PERIODICALLY shopped at a discount clothier for suits, because they have a decent selection of garments from some of the more popular designers. I regularly spent from $600.00 to $800.00 a year at this clothier. The most recent time I was there, the store was practically empty. I was wandering up and down several aisles, seeking the suit racks where my size was located. There were five sales people about ten feet away from me, absorbed in a conversation about their health-care benefits. Five indifferent types totally ignored me. Why did the store hire these guys if they don't understand the nature of their job? Why would a store hire them and not explain to them why they were on duty? Don't they understand their job is customer service? If they think it's just sales, they have it backwards. How can you sell anything if you don't offer customer service? Did they care if I walked out of the store?

I was getting angrier and angrier until I *did* walk out. As I passed by the "indifferent," not one of them said "Good-bye," no one tried to intervene to ask whether I needed assistance. How much revenue did they lose? Anywhere from $3,000.00 to over $4,000.00 over the next five years, since I will now take my business elsewhere for sure.

DOES ANYONE KNOW THE DEFINITION OF RECEPTIONIST?

MY CAR NEEDED to be serviced. The service advisor that was assigned to me is reliable and professional. Unfortunately, not all my communications with the dealer are through him. I decided to leave my car overnight for this routine maintenance—oil change, tire rotation, and fluid checks. The following morning when I walked into the dealer's service department, a technician instructed me to see the receptionist to complete the paperwork so that I could retrieve my car. When I arrived at her desk, she didn't bother to stop her administrative work, behaving as though it was more important than a real, live customer waiting to process a transaction. Finally, she allowed me the honor of her attention, at which point she curtly asked, "Name?" I told her. At that point, she pulled my paperwork from her pile, stamped it, and simply stated, "See the cashier."

Well, the dealership happens to be huge. I didn't know where the cashier was, and she hadn't even taken the small courtesy to point me in the right direction, behaving as though, if I couldn't locate the cashier, that was *my* problem. There was no, "Mr. Shapiro, we appreciate your business." Not even a simple, "Thank you." That such an indifferent type had the position of "receptionist" is unbelievable. *The very purpose of a receptionist is to welcome, greet, and show appreciation for a customer.* Could you imagine approaching the information desk of an airline or a tourist attraction with a question and getting a response like, "Beats me!" from the information guide? In a typical day, that receptionist probably speaks to a hundred customers. Can't this establishment find a welcomer that will make its customers advocates for its business, thereby potentially increasing business through word-of-mouth, rather than alienating customers—some of whom are bound to take their business elsewhere? The answer is to find a welcomer to occupy that position.

WATCHING THE LINE GETTING LONGER AND LONGER . . .

....

SEVERAL YEARS AGO, I went to a large, independently owned building-supply store. This regional chain has about fifteen stores. It was at the time when the two largest chains of this type were in the process of a nation-wide expansion. Well, the place had about fifteen checkout lanes, but only three or four were open, and each line was about ten people deep. Nearly half the customers (or would-be customers) simply left the store empty-handed after abandoning their items on a display counter or leaving their full shopping carts behind. This is common in understaffed stores. However in this case, five managers were facing a chaotic situation, but rather than do something to address the problem, they just watched. Whether they were managers in training or store personnel from a different branch is irrelevant. All they did was watch.

I'm a patient person, but not to the point where I will tolerate *total* incompetence. Neither is it my style to raise my voice. However, with only three or four checkout counters open, lines growing longer and longer, a management crew utterly passive and indifferent, I simply couldn't remain quiet about the fiasco I found myself in. At that point, I walked over to the group of dawdling managers.

"Instead of standing around, why don't you send or call someone to open up more counters!" I yelled. But it was to no avail. The group looked at me as though I were crazy. Would you stand patiently on line in such a situation? I hope not. If so, you may have become resigned to the fact that good customer service is simply rare these days. But there's no reason why you need to adapt this attitude.

WHY DO BUSINESS OWNERS FAIL TO SEE THE CONNECTION?

RECENTLY, I DECIDED to take a friend to a restaurant—one that has been in business for over twenty years and continues to have high ratings for food, service, and ambiance. However, when we arrived that evening, the maître d' barely said "Hello." Although it was a holiday weekend and the restaurant was only about one-third full, he did not ask us whether the table was acceptable. Had he asked, I would have suggested that we be seated in a more secluded area. My friend and I were catching-up on things, and it should have been apparent to anyone—not simply a restaurant professional—that we were not ready to order. But not to *this* waiter. He continually came over to us to inquire whether we had made our food selections. With each inquiry, he acted more annoyed. When we did order, the waiter acted utterly indifferent, as though he were "punishing" us for not being more prompt. Moreover, he showed no appreciation of the fact that we had selected his restaurant in which to dine in the first place. During the meal, he behaved impatiently, as though his main concern was that we leave so he could go off-duty. If you consider that it was a Friday evening, and that we completed our meal and left by 10:00 p.m., you would be hard put to claim we "overstayed our welcome." The coup de grace occurred as we walked out the door. There was the general manager standing outside on the sidewalk, talking on his cell phone. No good-bye, no thank you, no mention of an appreciation for our business. Has it reached the point that keeping a customer happy is just not that important anymore?

HOW ABOUT IF I CLEAN OFF MY DESK WHILE YOU ARE WAITING?

MY SON AND I encountered an indifferent at my bank. A customer service representative was sitting alone at her desk. She noticed us, but failed to ask how she could help us or even explain that another representative would assist us. Was she in the midst of finishing a report or a transaction? No. She casually straightened out her files, retrieved a bottle of Windex from her desk, and proceeded to clean it. Then she got up, left her work area, and returned with her lunch. Perhaps she was famished, and had to eat a quick lunch at her desk. Well, no. She then made a phone call, and began a friendly chat. After ten minutes of watching her on the phone, my son and I finally got up and asked, "Is there someone available to help us?" Her expression was one of annoyance, and her response was curt. "Someone else will be with you shortly," she said. What a show of appreciation for a long-time customer!

I just don't get it. This associate was clearly responsible for assisting bank patrons. Her work area indicated she was either a manager or assistant manager. I'm not suggesting that I should be treated better than another customer. However, there's no excuse for such indifference.

The indifferent type may not offer any information whatsoever. A welcomer will provide helpful information before you even ask. Isn't it worth an explanation of less than a minute to make a customer feel at ease? It's certainly worth the time to assure that I keep my account at the bank, and not the one across the street. The only reason I didn't consider taking my business elsewhere after my encounter was that my son and I were actually entertained by the indifferent representative. Maybe I should send her a thank you note for providing a perfect example of how just one staff member can undermine a business through unbecoming behavior.

There have many books written over the years about negative customer experiences. My purpose in adding to this list on un-customer-service-friendly encounters is to further support my premise that businesses don't seem to get the connection between customer service and the generation of repeat business. All of the stories relayed in this chapter would be perfect fodder for social media postings. And, unfortunately for the companies, they would all be negative in nature. Can you imagine if, in each of these situations, a welcomer had magically appeared? I can assure you that the outcome would have been dramatically different.

Demonstrating My Business Is Valuable While Waiting

"Good afternoon, gentlemen. So happy to see you. I'm the bank manager. I was scheduled to leave fifteen minutes ago because I have to pick up my daughter at school. I want you know that Brian is authorized to help you with any of your banking needs or concerns. He is just finishing up with another customer. Your wait will be no longer than five minutes. Meanwhile, would you like to help yourself to some coffee? Our coffee station is just around the corner from Brian's desk."

POWER POINTS WORTH REPEATING

- Businesses lose millions and millions of dollars each day because they don't understand how important it is to make a good first impression.
- Unfortunately, most non-welcomers don't have a holistic view of a customer. To them, the customer is simply a one-time transaction.
- When a customer needs to be transferred, it's a specific encounter that frequently is not handled in a manner that makes the customer feel valued and important.
- Being engaged so that he or she feels appreciated, the consumer has a greater likelihood of recalling the store representative *and* the particular store.
- Too many businesses don't get the connection between having non-welcomers and not generating sufficient repeat business to stay in business over the long haul.

4

Don't Just Answer My Question: Explain Your Answer

AS A CONSUMER, an observer of other consumers, and a professional researcher, I have discovered that, when you provide information that goes beyond just answering a question, people feel more comfortable and satisfied with the service interaction. This is just common sense. A welcomer will never simply provide a brief "yes" or no" response to an inquiry. For example, if you call a restaurant and ask to book a reservation for a particular time and day that is not available, a welcomer will not just say, "Sorry, we have nothing in that time slot." First, she will express how happy she is that you called for a reservation in the first place. Then she will ask whether another day or time might work. She also might advise the customer that since their restaurant gets booked quickly, he or she should call a week before to guarantee a reservation. She may even recommend to customers that are new to the area that they ask for the welcomer by name should they dine at the restaurant. That may seem like a lot to do during an initial telephone conversation, but not for a welcomer. That's what makes them welcomers. Why would you not place a welcomer in the role of creating a connection between your establishment and its most important asset: the customers? Being helpful, getting to know me, showing me that you care are all activities that demonstrate you are treating me as a person, not simply a person with a question.

One of the most vivid examples I can think of in describing how a true welcomer provides information that goes beyond the basics is when a pilot provides his passengers updates regarding a flight delay. Some pilots provide virtually no information

Putting Passengers at Ease

"I just heard from air traffic control that our flight is going to be delayed. They are saying this is due to weather conditions in New York, but they expect to release our plane within the next thirty minutes. I'm going to request an update in ten minutes, if I don't hear back from them. Either way, you'll get an update ten minutes from now. Although the doors are closed, you may use your cell phones for the next five minutes. I checked with other pilots who were waiting for clearance to take off, and they've reported an average twenty- to thirty-minute delay, so I feel comfortable that my estimate is accurate."

other than to say, "We have not received clearance to take off," while others offer extremely detailed information. Now while it's true that everyone wants and expects a pilot to be technically competent at flying a plane, a pilot that is an expert flyer and a welcomer is a real plus.

By providing extended information, the pilot is alleviating the passengers' anxieties by demonstrating that he or she is on top of the situation. A considerate pilot realizes that people who fly are frequently uneasy and uncomfortable, may have people waiting for them at their destination, and may be on a tight schedule. The pilot is treating you as a person first and not just a customer or a passenger. He knows people have concerns.

On every service interaction, representatives should try to provide useful information in addition to a simple catalogue of facts. If you are a bank manager, and a holiday is approaching, you may want to instruct tellers and call-center representatives to inform customers of early closings or other schedule changes. You may want to let them know that, as of the first of next month, the bank is planning to issue a new certificate of deposit instrument. Based on the banking habits of a bank customer, you may suggest that bank representatives recommend an account that has provisions more appropriate for a customer's current needs. If you have a bank teller who is a welcomer, I can almost guarantee that he will learn far more about each customer than a name and account number. He will know the type of work you do, how often you frequent the bank, which days you're most likely to do your banking, and even know of some of the other businesses you frequent in the area. I was completing a transaction with a teller (an obvious welcomer) who told me of a nearby supermarket where I could deposit my change and receive a gift certificate from the supermarket for 20 percent off the total amount of the transaction. If you had welcomers in all these front-line positions, customers would not simply perceive them as the people who handled their money transactions, but people from whom they could seek advice, because they've established trust.

The owner of a restaurant you frequent might decide to close his establishment for a vacation. Imagine how irksome it would be to drop by the restaurant only to find a sign stating, "Closed. Will re-open next Tuesday." Now, think of how you'd react if the owner and staff began alerting customers a month prior that the restaurant would be closed for a week the following month because the owner and his family will be visiting his mother for Mother's Day. Instead of ending up with a group of irate diners, the owner is more likely to receive words of praise for placing family matters before business. In this case, the additional information is not only useful for the patron at the time, it could enhance the restaurant's business in the future.

NOTHING WORSE THAN THREE-DAY-OLD FISH

I VISITED THE deli in my local grocery store to purchase some fish. I asked William, the regular counter person (and the welcomer I had previously mentioned), whether the fish would still be fresh on the second day. William didn't simply respond with a one-word "yes." He told me that the fish had just been prepared, and would taste as fresh the next day as it would that evening. I asked William to recommend a good cheese. He pointed out the differences among the various cheeses, identified their country of origin and which ones he could grate for me. He did not just answer my question. He gave me a thorough and detailed explanation. The more you explain, the more valued the customer feels. Extra time and attention goes a long way.

HONESTY REINFORCES REPEAT BUSINESS

ONE OF MY hobbies is collecting antique advertising memorabilia. I commonly go to antique shows, malls, and, of course, when appropriate, the old new standby, eBay. Part of the enjoyment I get from this hobby is the opportunity to hold an item, not simply see its photograph. When I ask to see a piece, for example, in a showcase, the more information I learn about the item the more I'm apt to buy it. If the explanation is accurate and thorough, there is a greater chance that I will purchase it. Several months ago, I was interested in an unusual antique bowl made of exquisite green glass. The dealer revealed that there was a hairline crack in the piece.

It's a Two-Way Street

A welcomer sees the person first, then the customer. Conversely, customers of welcomers see the welcomer as a person first and not just as an associate of your establishment. It's a two-way street, one lined with smiles, good will, and meaningful conversation.

I decided not to purchase it, but because the dealer was honest and described the piece comprehensively, I trust him and plan to pay him a visit in the future.

ANTICIPATE FUTURE NEEDS

WHILE RESEARCHING THIS book, I went to a store that sells storage containers. I had heard that this establishment was known for hiring talented associates and wanted to find out if this was accurate. I did learn that the store understood the value of providing information in far more depth than a quick answer to a question. When an associate approached to assist me, I told him that I did not have anything particular in mind, but I liked their store and wanted to see what new items they were stocking. Instead of responding with a smile or a short acknowledgement like "that's nice," he explained that if I picked up a Thursday edition of the local paper, I would find the store's ad, which contained information about their new merchandise. His response indicated that he had really listened to what I said. This is how you make

To Help or Not to Help: That Is the Answer

Customers appreciate when sales and service providers try their best to help customers. For those who really understand the definition of sales, it's not "selling" someone something, it's *helping* someone to find something he or she needs or wants. Welcomers have a history of helping people, that's why they make the best service and sales associates.

customers feel they are valued, something a robot wouldn't think of doing, because robots rarely consider what other information might be helpful to you. They might greet you with "canned" information, for example, "everything in the store is on sale this week," but this is directed towards the "generic" customer. Chances are a robot repeats the same information to everyone who walks through the door.

THE FRED ASTAIRE OF SERVICE

MY COUSIN, JUDD, who lives in our nation's capital, recently came for a visit, and the first thing he said when he arrived with his family was the following: "I'm absolutely desperate for a good New York hot pastrami sandwich." Now, I know one block in New York's garment district with about ten excellent delis. Each serves over-sized and delicious (albeit not healthful), hot pastrami sandwiches with all the fixings.

The waiter who served us was definitely a welcomer. He was meticulous in making sure we were served exactly what we ordered, and how we wanted it prepared. My cousin had requested that his home fries be well done. When Jimmy brought out the main courses, my cousin's was not among them. Jimmy explained that the cook was making sure the potatoes were prepared precisely as my cousin ordered them. Those who had requested a particular condiment received it exactly as requested: on the sandwich or on the side. Someone requested an extra spoon for the dessert. Jimmy made the spoon appear like magic. He was like the Fred Astaire of service. When he presented the check, he explained that we should pay at the front counter. He also alerted us that the restaurant did not accept credit or debit cards. He added that if we didn't have enough cash on hand, we could use the ATM in the restaurant. If you're thinking, "So what? These are just minor conveniences," think again. Yes, Jimmy was taking care of the little things. But Jimmy's demonstration of courtesy, helpfulness, and appreciation for our business bespeak an attitude of concern that is rare. Small things do make a difference. The fact that I recall just how well Jimmy treated us demonstrates the impact such little things can make.

PUMPING GAS, PROVIDING INFORMATION

ON ONE OCCASION, I pulled into my local gas station, just as another customer drove in at the same time. She asked the attendant if the garage could fix her tire, which seemed to be leaking air. The attendant suggested that she pull over to the air machine, inflate her tire, and leave the car if she could. Then, when the service station was less busy, they would check out her problem and have the car ready for her in the afternoon. He even asked her what time would be convenient for her to pick up her car, so the job would be completed by the time she

One Word Answers Could Be Reducing Your Revenues

Millions of dollars are lost every year by sales and service people who "answer" questions *correctly*, but not *effectively*, from a business standpoint. If you want to have a successful and profitable business, you need to have welcomers on the front lines.

returned. And if, of course, she had someone who could pick her up and bring her back when the repair had been completed.

The attendant *could* have answered her question with "No," or "We're too busy." These responses would be the truth, but would they encourage a connection? Simply stating a fact does not automatically mean you are being helpful. Do you think that a potential customer would ever become a paying customer? Of course not.

At the very least, you should train associates that one-word answers are not acceptable. Even referring a customer to a store that stocks an item you may not carry is preferable to a curt, "No, we don't sell that." Don't conclude that providing such information means you're losing business. In fact, it's one of the

Was Kris Kringle a Welcomer?

Nearly everyone loves the movie *Miracle on 34th Street*. In it, Kris Kringle is reprimanded for referring a Macy's customer to another store, where the shopper could find a special toy fire engine. Of course, Kris knew where to buy this unique item, since he was the real Santa Claus. When other customers hear about the story, Macy's receives thousands of letters complimenting Mr. Macy on the store's "new" policy. Mr. Macy then explains that Macy's will now be known for the store with a heart. And that's what businesses need to understand: that every store has merchandise, but very few make their customers feel appreciated, valued, and important. Welcomers innately know how to deliver service with their hearts, and this is reflected in their actions. And, yes, Kris Kringle was clearly a welcomer!

best ways to create and build loyalty. It shows the customer that you consider him a person first and a customer second.

Remember that the word "no" is a complete turn-off to a customer. Welcomers know this implicitly. They understand that short, close-ended responses result in a loss of business and dismayed customers. But don't take my word for it. The next time you ask a question of a salesperson or customer-service person, consider how *you* feel if you get an indifferent, negative response.

WHY HAVING A LOYALTY CARD IS JUST NOT ENOUGH

ONE DAY I ran out of toner for my printer, so I went to a branch of a national office-supply store to purchase a new cartridge. As I waited to make my purchase, the woman ahead of me, who had also purchased some items in the store, was explaining to the young man at the counter that she had recently signed up for the store's loyalty program but never

---

Questions/Concerns Are Great Opportunities to Make a Customer Connection

When a customer asks a question or brings up a concern, a salesperson has a great opportunity to connect with him or her. This can solidify the customer's relationship with the store, and even help generate more business if your customer becomes an advocate as well, and it brings in new customers. Consider how much business could be lost (or gained), depending on whether a customer has a transaction with a welcomer rather than a robot.

received a rewards check in the mail. Consider the situation. If the customer was a member of the store's rewards program, it was nearly certain she was a regular customer. The very purpose of these programs is to cultivate return customers. While such programs may provide such an incentive, if a company focused on hiring welcomers, there probably wouldn't be a need for them.

The young man told the customer that it was "possible" that she did not receive the rewards check because she "may not have" accumulated the minimum sales dollars to qualify. The woman did not seem very satisfied with this response. Can you consider why? After all, the salesperson was providing a reasonable answer. Reasonable, yes, but engaging? Definitely not! A good sales associate wouldn't use terms like "possible" or "may not have." The action the employee should have taken would have been to check the customer's account to see if that was indeed the reason. If he couldn't locate the information while she was in the store, he should have offered to contact her the next day for a definitive answer. Taking that extra step indicates that the customer's request is important, and that the customer's business is appreciated. If this customer spent an average of $500.00 a year on office supplies, and took her business elsewhere, over a five-year period the lost business would amount to $2,500.00.

PROVIDING ADDITIONAL INFORMATION CAN BE COOL

ONE HOT, SUMMER day, my son and I went into a New York café. He was wearing a suit. The hostess offered us the option of an indoor table or one outside on the restaurant's patio. My son said he much preferred a table inside since he wanted to stay cool. The hostess not only found us a comfortable table in the air-conditioned section, but offered us a seat right under the air conditioning duct—the coolest area in the place. Very cool indeed! Our hostess was a natural welcomer. This was evident the moment she greeted us with a warm, enthusiastic smile, when she listened attentively to our request, and went "beyond the call of duty" by explaining which area of the café was the coolest. Additionally, to demonstrate how her behavior supports my claim that explanations are far superior to simple responses, she took the time to explain why she thought we'd prefer the table she suggested. Through this personal engagement, she was helping to build loyalty among her first-time customers.

In the following chapter, I describe in detail how a robot-acting associate can be taught to think, act and say things that would be more welcoming and helpful to the customer. It's really difficult to help a customer unless you understand his or her needs. As I mentioned in the introduction, asking the

Wanting to Help Is Deep-Rooted

Welcomers have a history of helping others—often dating back to their childhoods. They know their job is to help people, and you can't truly help someone without getting to know something about him first. How can you learn anything about a customer or expect a customer to remember you or your business if you respond to him with answers that discourage engagement and connection? The simple answer is that you *can't!*

consumer appropriate questions, not only provides information to better service the customer, it equally helps establish a dialogue or a connection, which will result in repeat sales. Asking consumers when they first walk into your store, "How can I help you today?" is something that just sounds too robotic and many times will solicit a response such as "I'm just looking" or "Not sure" or "Show me where I can find the bedding department." Those types of questions tend not to create that connection you need to secure a repeat customer. A welcomer will automatically engage the consumer before trying to assist him with his specific inquiry. A welcomer will notice what the customer is wearing, maybe that she is wet from an unexpected storm, in a hurry, just stopped in unexpectedly or seems to be familiar with the store.

Customers also appreciate when associates provide additional helpful information about their intended purchases, whether that information persuades or dissuades the customer from making a purchase that day. I know as a customer that, as a general rule, the more I know about the product or service in advance of the purchase, the greater the chance that the store will earn my repeat business. No one really wants to spend his hard-earned dollars on a business that doesn't care enough about its customers and doesn't spend the time to teach the consumer something useful that he may have not known before.

Seeing the Customer as a Person First

A welcomer will engage the customer in a dialogue, which will clearly demonstrate to the customer that the associate sees him or her as a person first, a customer second.

POWER POINTS WORTH REPEATING

- A welcomer will never simply provide a brief "yes" or "no" response to an inquiry.
- Being helpful, getting to know the customer, showing him or her that you care, are all activities that demonstrate you are treating the customer as a person, not simply a person with a question.
- Millions of dollars are lost every year by sales and service people who "answer" questions *correctly*, but not *effectively*, from a business standpoint.
- Customers of welcomers see the welcomer as a person first and not just as an associate of your establishment. It's a two-way street.
- For those who really understand the definition of sales—it's not "selling" someone something, it's *helping* someone to find something he or she needs or wants.
- Small things do make a difference in servicing a customer; customers appreciate it when they learn something they didn't know before.

5

Can a Robot Become a Welcomer? Your Final Answer, Please

THE PREMISE OF this book is that, if you want to truly develop a strong sales and service component of your business, you need to find some welcomers, because they make the ideal associates. They have an innate trait of viewing customers as people first and consumers second. They automatically make people feel important, appreciated, and valued. From my experience, this people-to-people, person-to-person interaction has the potential to turn an initial contact into a customer-retention journey that will last for as long as your customer is a shopper.

Unfortunately, the percentage of *natural* welcomers is not as large as that of robots, but they *do* exist. Given that fact, why wouldn't a business manager or owner jump at the chance to hire a welcomer, or move an associate currently working for the company who is one into a front-line service position? I'm not writing this book to discover the reason. But I am writing this book so that the business community has the information and motivation to find these folks with these innate skills and place them in the most critical sales and service positions, where they can directly interact with your most valuable asset, your customers.

Many businesses may already have these "Doctors of First Impressions" in their employ but not in front-line positions. They may be performing back-office functions: some pulling merchandise for shipping, others entering data into their company's database systems. If you are a manager or an owner of a business, first look at your current associates to see if you can find one of these gems. If you don't have enough welcomers (and probably nobody can have enough), start the search now.

Let's remind ourselves that all welcomers appear to have the desire and ability to help. They help put a smile on someone's face. They will

Wired and Dangerous

In Chip Bell and John Patterson's best-selling book, *Wired and Dangerous— How Your Customers Have Changed and What to Do about It*, they state: "Customers love it when you tell them you appreciate their business. They never forget they have options and they feel valued when you show you never forgot that either. Sound enthusiastic! If you sound like a "thank-you-for-shopping-at-J-Mart" robot, they will remember your insincerity, not your gratitude. Be a joy carrier. If you give your customers the best you have, the best will come back to you!

help someone find the perfect gift for a best friend. They have such a strong impulse to help that they might tell customers that they'll find exactly what they're looking for at your competitor's business on the next block. In my research, I've found that welcomers have a history of helping. It's not an impulse that begins when they start a service or sales position. They want to help people today, and even more important, look forward to helping them tomorrow too!

SAYING "HELLO" TO MORE THAN ONE CUSTOMER AT A TIME

A WHILE AGO, I had found a Doctor of First Impressions at one of the larger pharmacy chains near my apartment. I have been a customer of this particular pharmacy location for at least a year, and never ran into any welcomers. Every person at the individual check-out counters has been robotic. But on this day, as soon as I walked up to the counter, a newly-hired associate, Carmen, gave me the biggest smile, and said, "How are you doing today?" Carmen didn't ask the question robotically. Her smile, her demeanor, and the little twinkles in her eye indicated she really wanted to know. It was an instant connection. Then she said, "Have a good day. It's beautiful out." It was obvious that she directed the statement to me, not a generic customer.

Two days later, when I realized I hadn't picked up shaving cream, I dropped by the same store to purchase a tube. I wasn't able to wait in Carmen's line, but I did end up at the register next to hers. I looked over and our eyes connected.

"How are you doing today?" she said, a big smile on her face. I thought, "I wasn't even standing in her line, but she saw one of her customers in another line and just naturally said "Hello." I was surprised at first, but then I understood there wasn't anything to be mystified about. That's what a welcomer does—takes in everyone in her field of vision as she works. As Carmen was helping the customer in her particular check-out line, she was asking him if he found everything that he was looking for. When he said that he couldn't find a certain brand of shampoo, Carmen just didn't say, "Sorry," she jumped over the check-out partition as if she were in a pole vaulting contest and said to her customer, "I know exactly where it is, let's go find it together."

All I could do was look on in amazement as my inner voice said, "Wow! Wow! Wow!" The reason that I'm relating this story now is to remind readers that are in a position to look for and hire welcomers (and those that can recommend welcomers), that

Do Welcomers Learn How to Be Welcomers from Their Parents?

Many welcomers I interviewed had memories of how their parents were always generous, considerate, and helpful to anyone that had less than they. This generosity might take the form of collecting food donations, manning soup kitchens, volunteering to coach young children, and so on. Jo Ann, one welcomer I met, was the youngest child of four and had three older brothers that she adored, and, in turn, they adored her back. She used to do anything she could to help them out when she was growing up. Of course, she wanted them to take her along whenever they were going someplace cool or new. Today, Jo Ann just has the desire to help people, whether they are cherished friends or someone she has just met at a supermarket.

every welcomer that I've met or that I've had an opportunity to find out about had a history of helping people. Carmen catapulted over the check-out counter because she wanted to help the customer find what he was looking for. She just didn't say, "The shampoo is in Aisle Six on the right-hand side." She literally took the gentleman's hand, led him to the exact spot where the shampoo was shelved, and brought him back to the check-out counter. You can be sure her customer was well on his retention journey of a lifetime.

So if you own or manage a business—before doing a search to hire a welcomer—see if there are any hidden in the back office. If you find that no one on staff fits the bill, make sure that, when you have your next opening for a front-line position, you hire someone with a history of helping people. Helpful people belong in customer service: that's what customer service is all about—helping people find what they need.

There is something else you can do to help your business create a welcoming environment for customers: seek out those robots that may be welcomer-wannabees. Who are these folks, and how do you identify them? While researching this book, I did a great deal of observing, listening, and thinking. I know that there are a large number of robot-like sales and service providers that want to do the best job that they can assisting customers. One motivation may be that they want their employers to be happy with their performance. That's a perfectly good incentive. After all, who doesn't want her boss to like her, or at the very least, respect her value to a company?

In describing these welcomer-wannabees, I had originally planned to include a section on how they might work at developing a relationship with *their* customers. However, after reflection, I realized that to use the term "their customers" in the context of welcomer-wannabees was an anomaly. Natural welcomers think of the person they're helping as someone with whom to build a relationship. Unfortunately, welcomer-wannabees don't readily see the relationship part. While they don't necessarily see a customer as a widget (as many sales and service people do), they do see the customer as just another transaction—indistinguishable from the one before or the one to follow. On the other hand, welcomers see the people they assist as *their* customers. That means that they know basic facts about them, for example, their names, something about their families, and perhaps what part of town they reside in. Additionally, they know something about their buying habits: whether they're regular or repeat customers, their likes and dislikes regarding

certain products, what they're willing to pay for an item, and so on. I should mention that they don't collect this information the way a customer survey might (for example, the kind you get when filling out the warranty form for a newly purchased product) to create marketing strategies. They do it because they naturally want to build relationships and connections. But think about it. Can there be a better marketing technique than that?

How Does a Welcomer Think?

When a welcomer sees someone walk through the door that is one of "her" customers, her first thought is the following: "I wonder how he is doing today?" or "How did she like the concert she attended last week?" or "I can't wait to tell him about my upcoming vacation?" She's *not* thinking, "I wonder what he is looking for today?"

Can a Robot Become a Welcomer? Your Final Answer, Ple

106

There is no doubt that an associate who tends to act can care about customers and treat them with courtesy a professionalism. However, the robotic associate cannot m quantum leap in thinking and behaving that comes naturally to the welcomer: that the customer is a person first, and a customer second. A welcomer treats the customer in a sales or service transaction this way because the welcomer *perceives* him or her this way. In so many retail and service establishments, customers can feel they've received the product or service they wanted. Afterwards, they can view the transaction as one where they were helped by a professional whom they respected and trusted, because robotic individuals can know all "technical" aspects of the job and fulfill their obligation as well as anyone. But what they haven't done is make a *connection.*

Let me give you one example before we move on.

EARNING REPEAT BUSINESS

FOR ME, RENTING a bungalow for a week during the summer is not just a matter of rest and relaxation. It affords my family and

It's All About the Connection

It's the connection that will provide the consumer with that magical feeling that, "Hey, that person was special. I got to know her (or him) almost instantly and he got to know about me as well." When the customer thinks about the transaction, the individual comes to mind, not just his or her efficiency. That's a big difference. In other words, the customer understands that a "real" person is there to help, not the company the person works for.

me time to be together for an extended period, to relax, laugh, share stories, and just get to talk to one another. I look forward to this ritual every year. Now that my kids are in their twenties, this once-a-year gathering becomes even more important. One of the daily activities is to make dinner together or go out to a restaurant as a family, usually alternating the two, because both are enjoyable. Our shore town and its bordering neighborhoods have about twenty good restaurants that offer special seafood (naturally) dishes daily.

It was while sampling a new restaurant that we met a terrific welcomer, Gary. Gary was working as a waiter for the summer. In the fall, he was returning to his studies to become a hospital technician. How did we learn that? Gary was engaging. He asked us if this was our first visit to the restaurant, and when we told him it was, he followed up by inquiring why we happened to choose it on that particular day. Before we realized it, we now had another member of our family at the restaurant. The difference was that he wasn't sitting at our table. You might think that perhaps because it was our first visit or because we were on vacation or because Gary was still in school that made him particularly friendly. But my

Communicating to the Customer You Want Him to Return

"Mr. Shapiro, I'm so glad you dined at the restaurant this evening," he said as he handed me the check. "I really enjoyed having a nice conversation with you and your family. Since you're going to be down here for another few days or so, feel free to come back and visit. It would be a pleasure to see you and your family before I head back to school."

intuition said otherwise. I just knew Gary was being Gary. He saw us as people. My family could see from my expression that I was interacting with a welcomer, and, as if reading my mind, they nodded in assent.

In the ninety minutes we spent dining, Gary had learned (and remembered!) the following: how long we were on vacation, what I did for a living, and where my sons resided, among other things. The food was excellent. The service was good, and the place had a nice ambiance, but what made us go back *two* more times within the next six days was Gary. He was a welcomer!

So what I'm saying is, if you are not a welcomer and care about your business, try to get to know your customers along the way—as people. Find out what got them there in the first place. That could be a great way to understand them as living, breathing people, not just names in a computer database.

These are things a welcomer would naturally learn over time, or even immediately. If you think that you may have many robots who really would like to act and think as a welcomer does, it's important to understand that information is the key. The more you know about a person, the better sales or customer service experience you will deliver. And the better you know the individual as a person, and not just as a customer, the greater motivation the customer will have to go out of his way to do business at your establishment rather

There Is More than Just Delivering Good Service

Good customer service is good for today. Having a welcomer provide good customer service will make you return tomorrow. That's a big difference.

your competitor's. While I addressed a potential concern about asking customers questions to get to know them better in the introduction, I think it is important to stress the difference between being nosy and trying to assist someone by getting to know her better. And, as in any situation, there will be some people who will not wish to have a dialogue with anyone, but in my experience those tend to be rare occurrences. As I also mentioned previously, even a genuine and welcoming smile can get a customer to automatically want to connect with one of your associates. It's a simple concept.

The primary audience for this book is owners and managers of businesses. The businesses could be for profit, charitable, in the healthcare industry, or something else. The principals outlined in this book are universal; they are simple to comprehend and easy to implement. If you can find welcomers you will need to provide them with little training on how to be more *welcoming*. You need to train welcomers on your particular brands, your policies, and your

Getting to Know Your Customers as People First

- How did you hear about our establishment?
- Did you hear from neighbors about our store, and if so, what did you hear?
- What do you need today that made you go shopping?
- Why did you make a special effort to come out in this hot weather or rain to buy something?
- Do you have a special occasion coming up?
- Have you been in the store before?
- Did you grow up in this area or someplace else?

company's philosophies, but not on how to provide excellent customer service. Welcomers will view your customers as people first, customers second, *naturally.*

During my research for my book, I interviewed hundreds of welcomers whom I met throughout my travels, so I have proof that they do exist. But, I have to admit that the percentages of welcomers I have discovered is certainly smaller than the numbers of robots I encountered. The good news is that I am a strong believer that training works. I'm confident that, if businesses train their robot-acting sales and service associates on how a welcomer views the customer, a large percentage of robots will be able to deliver service that will encourage more repeat customers. However, similar to other training initiatives, the people in the training program need to grasp the tools and see the benefits to the customer, the company, and to themselves. Therefore, if you have robots who want to be more like welcomers, I have named this robot subset, welcomer-wannabees.

What kind of training tools do welcomer-wannabees need to act and think like welcomers?

The Whole Is Greater than the Sum of the Parts

Aristotle, the famed Greek philosopher, scientist, and educator, is responsible for first developing the axiom, "The whole is greater than the sum of the parts." Taking into account this wisdom, we can say that, while each of the three elements in a welcomer-wannabees tool kit is of equal importance, when used together, the customer's experience will dramatically improve. Another way of saying this is that they operate synergistically.

The training tool kit will be segmented into three distinct compartments: *the greet, the assist,* and *the leave-behind.* These three components will help you unlock the secrets of repeat business. Training welcomer-wannabees on how welcomers act and think will increase your business's welcomers and, in turn, create additional business opportunities.

THE GREET

LET'S TAKE THE first component: *the greet. The greet* is essential and important, and Doctors of First Impressions do it naturally without any need for a tool kit. When a welcomer sees a first-time customer or his or her customer, the welcomer provides a big "happy to see you" smile. So my first suggestion for welcomer-wannabees is to do the same. Regardless of whether you work at a check-out counter, a bank-teller window, or a call center, give a big "Hello" and a smile. You can't see a smile via telephone, but it will positively affect the way you communicate. If a welcomer knows a customer's name, he or she will use the name. It's as simple as saying, "Mr. Jameson, how are you today?"

Why is that first moment of contact so significant? Let's consider the importance of first impressions. A first impression begins the second you interact with someone. The way you greet a customer sets the stage for the entire interaction. So, my advice to welcomer-wannabees is that, when you see a customer walk through the door, think how you'd act if he or she were a close friend you hadn't seen for a while. You wouldn't ask your best friend, "How can I help you?" in a monotone, robotic manner.

I'm amazed how I can go to the same deli each week and be waited on by the same associate, and the person seems to have never laid eyes on me before. For many local neighborhood businesses, most shoppers are repeat customers. So when you are initiating interactions with consumers, give them a "Hello" exactly as though they're loyal customers. If they aren't, there's a good chance they'll become loyal.

When you are standing behind the counter or at a hostess station, you can say "Hello" to more than once person at a time. There is no rule that a "Hello" can only be communicated to the first person in line. Remember Carmen, who said "Hi" to me, even though I wasn't standing in her line.

Welcomers are observant. And welcomer-wannabees need to pay better attention to what the customer is holding, wearing, using, and so forth.

WHAT CAN YOU TELL FROM A SHOPPING BAG?

ALTHOUGH I CONSIDER myself to have at least average intelligence, when it comes to learning languages other than English, I have never had too much success. I took four years of French in high school and don't remember even one word. I took one year of Spanish in college and barely passed the course. But, I'm also one not to give up easily. So, I'm back to learning Spanish. I was meeting a friend for lunch in a mall near his home

Let's Start the Greet with a Big Hello

In this era of technology, people are more stressed than ever. Getting that big and warm hello can go a long way in this age of daily technology changes, multi-tasking, and high anxiety environments.

in New Jersey and decided that I would stop by a Rosetta Stone kiosk just prior to meeting my friend at noon. At lunch I had my shopping bag on the chair next to where I was sitting. The waitress came over to introduce herself. Her name was Nancy. She started the conversation by saying, "I see someone is trying to learn Spanish" (obviously noticing what was sticking out of my shopping bag). After five minutes of a dialogue, Nancy found out all about the book idea and my friend and I found out that Nancy was working at this restaurant part-time while going to medical school. It just made the entire experience more enjoyable. Of course, welcomers or welcomer-wannabees need to be careful not to mention something that they noticed of a private nature, but welcomers naturally pay attention.

I have related the story of how my wife Shelley, while at an exhibit booth, would compliment a women about a beautiful pin or scarf, or say to a gentleman, "I love your tie." People like to be complimented. Welcomers notice the person first, before they ever view him as a customer. And, part of that noticing is seeing what the person is wearing, her general frame of mind, what he might be carrying, and so forth. It's a great way to engage a customer to get to know her better.

If welcomer-wannabees want to sound like welcomers over the phone, they need to think like welcomers. How can you do that? Think about simply seeing on the caller ID that your best friend is calling you. How would you say "Hello?" I'm sure it would be with enthusiasm and interest. That is the way all calls should be answered. As I have mentioned many times, in so many cases, a company has one opportunity to turn that one interaction with a customer into a lifetime advocate for its service or product. Do not miss that opportunity. Answer every call with a big, warm "Hello."

Let's look at an example of how a welcomer responds to a customer who calls about an upcoming sales event over the phone. Note how a welcomer can turn a person that randomly calls a faceless place of business into a customer that is one of their own. The anonymous business now becomes a site the consumer looks forward to contacting. When a welcomer starts the first-time shopper on the road to becoming a repeat customer, the image of your business transforms from a generic, impersonal institution to a company with a human face and voice. Here is the way it happens:

MARY (WELCOMER): Hi, this is Mary. How can I help you today? (warm, friendly, and with a smile in her voice)

CALLER (POTENTIAL CUSTOMER): I was wondering if your sale has started yet, and, if it hasn't, do you know when it will start?

MARY: I can certainly help you with that. I know that some items are on sale, but not in all departments. If you can give me your name and telephone number, I can check with the manager and get back to you. She is not in until 3:00 p.m. today. May I have a contact number?

CALLER: Sure, my name is Barbara, and the best number to reach me at is 555-626-4444.

MARY: May I reach you at that number any time today?

CALLER: Most definitely. It's my cell phone, and I'll have it on all day.

MARY: Barbara, thanks for calling. I will be sure to get back to you after 3:00. If you are not available to answer the phone, I will leave a detailed message. But Barbara, if you need more information, just call back and ask for Mary. These are my hours and it would be great to meet you whatever day you make it in.

[handwritten margin note:] Use their name

e greeting sets the stage for the rest of the transaction. It makes sense to make a person feel like you are *eager* to help her find what she needs before you actually assist her with what she needs.

THE ASSIST

THE NEXT COMPARTMENT in the tool kit is *the assist*. The assist includes helping the customer find what he needs; that is, handling his bank transaction, checking-out his items at the register, and so on. Let's assume that a welcomer-wannabee might already be knowledgeable about the stock, service, or the business policies. So how can the actual transaction sound more like that of a welcomer? If you were not able to ask the customer for her name during *the greet*, then find out during the assist. It's

Tools for the Greet

- Give a big hello as if you know the person.
- If you do recognize the person, and know his name, use the name; if you don't know his name, ask for it and try to remember it for the next visit.
- Next, tell him your name even if it is on your badge: "Hi, my name is Mary Associate."
- If you don't remember his name the next time you see him, say "I'm sorry, what's your name? I forget." He will feel really good that you tried to remember.
- Be aware of what customers are wearing, carrying, holding; compliment them if it's appropriate.
- Then ask, "How can I help you today?"

one of best ways to turn the customer into a person. When you find out the shopper's name and *use* it during the interaction, it makes the entire transaction more personable. It shows the customer that you are a good listener and that you want to personalize the conversation in addition to helping the customer get the information she seeks.

In Chapter 4, we provided the suggestion, "Don't just give me an answer; explain your answer." One of the largest opportunities for improving upon *the assist* is to provide additional useful information. The following story of my visit to a flower shop might provide a good example.

IF YOU WANT A PLANT TO THRIVE, YOU NEED ADDITIONAL USEFUL INFORMATION

ONE DAY, I needed a plant for my apartment and went to the famed flower district in New York, located on the Avenue of the Americas in the West Twenties. There you will find store after store, with all varieties of house plants, tropical plants, and flowers. I walked into one at random. There were a couple of associates preparing arrangements and pruning plants.

"What can we do for you?" one of the employees asked. "I'd like to buy a plant," I said, injecting a bit of wise-guy humor. As soon as I mentioned what I was looking for, they sprang into action. "José will be happy to help you," one of the associates said.

That was just the right thing to put me at ease. No one asked me about the type of plant I was looking for. No one asked me about how much I was willing to spend. When most people buy plants for their homes, unless they are plant aficionados, they

want advice. The customer wants to feel as though he or she is in
good hands. Some things most people need to know include how
often the plant should be watered, its lighting needs, whether it
requires special fertilizer, whether it needs to be repotted, and
so on. Quite a bit of information is required to assure that you
can maintain a healthy and attractive plant. Sometimes the best
advice doesn't work, but it certainly puts you at an advantage
over the alternative, which is not having a clue regarding how to
care for the plant.

When someone is buying a shirt, a pair of shoes, or a new
garden hose, if you think there is some additional useful
information the consumer might find valuable, simply
communicate it. It could be that the garden hose comes with
optional connectors, or that the shoes are also waterproof, or that
the shirt is available in different colors should the purchaser like
the shirt and decide to buy more. A Doctor of First Impressions
is so eager to help and has such a well-tuned intuition of
a customer's preferences that he provides the appropriate
information during the interaction.

I named the second compartment of the tool kit, *the assist*,
for a good reason. It has a two-fold purpose, with both aspects
being directly related. After many years of researching consumer
behaviors, I've found one of the primary drivers of overall
satisfaction is the degree to which the customer feels that he is
being helped. A person who knows how to help the customer
(1) may not always have the product the customer wants, (2)
can't move him up at the check-out counter, and (3) can't put
something on sale that is regular price. But, when a customer feels
that the associate is doing her best to help him, it matters. It's what
clearly differentiates one service or sales provider from another.

As we learned in prior chapters, one of the best ways to help a customer is to view him or her as a person first, a customer second.

Let's take a closer look at the three scenarios I mentioned in the above paragraph. In the first case, the customer may be looking for an item that is no longer in stock or is no longer available from the manufacturer. It makes a big difference from the consumer's perspective, on how he is handled and with what degree of helpfulness. If the item is out of stock, instead of making a robotic response such as "We no longer have that item in your size," a more helpful response might be "Let me check some of our other stores and get back to you later on today," or "Let me ask my manager when she arrives to see if she plans on placing a re-order," or even as Macy's did in *Miracle on 34th Street*, potentially suggest a competitor that may carry the same item.

During the holidays, check-out lines tend to be long, especially at certain times of the day. If someone is in a hurry, frustrated, and stressed by the time they reach your counter, certainly an acknowledgment that you are sorry that he had to wait so long will make the customer feel better. Perhaps if the customer needs the merchandise wrapped for a present, he can pay for it now and pick up the package later on in the day. There are definitely things that can be done that act and sound helpful to the customer.

Looking at the third scenario, I know that the welcomers who know me communicate as much information about a pending sale as they are allowed to offer. However, they may also point out that, although their sale normally occurs towards the end of June, if I wait until that time, the store may not have my particular size or color preference. I'm the kind of customer that loves options, and welcomers tend to present *their* customers with options that would be of interest to them, based on their preferences, which they have garnered over time.

Always try to have your associates avoid one-word answers by explaining or elaborating on your responses. Think of your favorite teacher and how the teacher would really go into detail on a subject he knew well, without referring to notes, a textbook, or a laptop. Finally, these details should not be provided as though they were on a list on a computer screen or in a catalogue.

When I first started to explain the reason why I named the second compartment *the assist,* I explained that it had a two-fold

Tools for the Assist

- Find out the customer's name if you don't already know it.
- Use the customer's name at least once during the interaction, but not more than twice.
- Tell her your name, even if it is on your badge.
- Try to determine the underlying emotion for the customer being upset, happy, angry, or frustrated; customers appreciate when you acknowledge what they are feeling, and, when appropriate, apologize for the extra wait, the long lines, the fact that you need to take time to check the stock, or what have you.
- Don't always say, "How can I help you?" but sometimes say, "I would like to help you with that. Do you mind if I ask you a few questions to better understand what you are looking for?"
- Don't give one-word answers; provide detailed explanations.
- Always provide additional useful information, such as "We have a Facebook page, a website, other stores, our annual sales," and so forth.

purpose; the first was that a major driver of a customer being satisfied with an interaction is the degree of helpfulness that the customer felt the associate offered. Since the overriding theme of all the welcomers I met through my travels was their desire to *help*, it's a perfect match. It's simple. Customers love when they get the extra help and welcomers love to provide it.

THE LEAVE-BEHIND

THE FINAL COMPARTMENT of the welcomer-wannabees tool kit is *the leave-behind. The leave-behind,* coupled with *the greet* and *the assist,* will allow any welcomer-wannabees to unlock the secrets of repeat business.

When the transaction is complete, you should always end with a return invitation. It doesn't matter whether you've just helped a customer select a new outfit, waited on him at a restaurant table, or processed his credit card at the gas pump. Say, "Mr. Jones, thanks for stopping in. I'm glad I was able to help you today. I would love to help you the next time you are in the area, or need one of our services or products. And please ask for me. I'm generally here from Tuesday

Tools for the Leave-Behind

- Thanking the customer for his business.
- Inviting the customer to return.
- Notifying the customer that, if possible, you would like to personally assist him again.
- Communicating your work schedule, direct line, and so on.
- And it's always nice to close with, "Mr. Shapiro, have a great day."

through Sunday, 1:00 pm to 8:00 p.m. Did you want me to write that down for you?"

If you think about it, doesn't it make sense that obtaining repeat business should include some kind of statement that makes the customer feel that you enjoyed helping him, that it was fun to get to know him and find out his tastes, and that you would personally like to see or talk to him again? It's the part of the transaction that rarely gets communicated, but it's so important. Most of Chapter 10 is devoted to the concept of *the leave-behind.*

If a welcomer-wannabee follows these steps, she will fulfill an important role in sales and service: engage today, communicate for tomorrow.

My goal is not to change the world, but to try to transform customer service, just one transaction at a time. If a robot-acting person keeps a tool kit filled with several welcomer tools and uses it every day, he or she will be amazed at what can happen. It will make the customers feel more important, appreciated, and valued. When the customer says, "Thanks for helping me today," it will make the sales or customer-service associate think, "Hey, not only did I help the

> ## Customer Service—New Rules for a Social Media World
>
> In Peter Shankman's exciting book, *Customer Service—New Rules for a Social Media World,* he talks about the acronym WARS, as a new way of thinking about the customer.
>
> - Make them feel Welcomed.
> - Make them feel Appreciated.
> - Make them want to Return.
> - Make them want to Share.

customer get what she came in for, I really feel good too." The function of a sales or service associate is to help the customer. Helping does not simply mean processing a credit card, telling the shopper what hours your store is open, or just showing him to his table. Helping is treating the customer as a person first and a consumer second.

Don't think of helping a customer as the end of a transaction, but as the start of a customer's lifelong retention journey.

POWER POINTS WORTH REPEATING

- There are a large number of robots who can be trained to act and think like welcomers.
- Welcomers want to help people today, and even more important, look forward to helping them tomorrow too!
- Many welcomers have vivid memories of how their parents were always generous, considerate, and helpful to anyone that had less than them.
- Those robots who are eager to become welcomer-wannabees can benefit from a tool kit that includes *the greet, the assist,* and *the leave-behind.*
- A critical component of repeat business is engaging the customer today and communicating about tomorrow.

6

....

I'm Standing in Line— Am I the Invisible Man?

CHECK-OUT LINES ARE everywhere: at the supermarket, at the bank, at electronics and cell phone stores, and, of course, at airline terminals, where appropriate procedures seem to be part of an endless national debate. With each new line that becomes a part of our routine, it seems we've added one more situation that inevitably turns into a frustrating experience. Many supermarkets, pharmacies, and department stores are attempting to address the problem by automating the check-out process, so that people may check out themselves. If you work for a company that has initiated this time-saving policy, or is considering it, you may end up being pennywise and dollar foolish. I understand that companies are attempting to save money, and perhaps reducing staff, but are the front lines the place where these strategies should be implemented?

In previous chapters, I've mentioned the "robot" styled salesperson or service provider.

And frankly, if you have check-out counters filled with robots, indifferent, or the hostile, these automated check-out counters are probably just as efficient and perhaps more customer friendly.

But let's consider what the result will be in the long run, from the perspective of the person waiting *in* the line. If a customer is greeted by a human robot, or an actual robotic scanning device, you've lost perhaps the only opportunity for human interaction, the only chance for the consumer to attach a friendly face or recall a helpful hand to his or her shopping experience. Instead, the person leaves the premises without any experience of human interaction. Consider what is going through the mind of this consumer. He or she isn't thinking about the friendly conversation he or she had with the cashier or teller. In fact, the people providing you with business most likely have *nothing* in mind, no face to connect or fond recollection for the next time.

The check-out line is potentially the only opportunity for an associate to create a customer relationship, but more and more frequently, businesses are ignoring this opportunity. The entire set-up, along with those markers that read "Next in line," "The line starts here," or "This lane is closed," are not customer friendly. They simply contribute to a transaction that treats customers as widgets. I'm sure you are familiar with the phrases, "Your card, please," "Credit or debit," or "Swipe the pad." Those phrases are uttered perfectly and efficiently, but how about saying, "Hello" and "Thank you"? These phrases are often expressed with all the sincerity of a self-serve kiosk. Banks, movie theatres, and pharmacies, among other businesses, rope off the line, creating a perfect metaphor for the conveyor belt. Unfortunately, it's the consumer that is being processed.

THE RETURN COUNTER

I DECIDED MY bathroom could use some new fluffy towels, washcloths, and a mat, so I went shopping in the household section of one of the largest department stores. I got home and began carefully reorganizing my bathroom's linen closet. It was then I discovered a brand new bath mat I had totally forgotten that I had purchased a while ago. The next day I was back at the store with the same mat I had purchased just twenty-four hours before. The customer service counter is easy to find—just to the left as you walk in.

At the counter, I told the store representative my dilemma, but before I even finished my sentence, "Receipt, please," the employee said mechanically. She scanned the item, circled a coded number on the receipt, and walked away. Fine. There's nothing wrong with efficiency. However, it would have been nice if she had said something . . . *anything* in fact. Was I getting a refund? Had she strutted away in order to call a store manager? That was in the realm of possibility, as I had absolutely no idea whether she was even planning to return. I wasn't sure if she was coming back or not. I made a deliberate turn of the head to see if I could spot her. There she was, several yards away talking to another associate. Was she discussing my bath mat? Was I acting suspicious? You see, because she was treating me as a humanoid widget, I had absolutely no idea what was going on. Then I realized that she had actually credited my card as she was circling the item, but of course never communicated that to me at all. It was as if I were totally invisible to her.

For retail stores, particularly large ones, the return counter is the perfect place to engage a customer—perfect owing to its placement and purpose. It could be essential to building a rapport with a customer, especially if the customer had a complaint about a product. I think it's just human nature to feel a bit slighted at purchasing the wrong item, or a badly fitting item, even if it's not the fault of the store. The worst strategy in terms of customer service or sales is to make the consumer feel even worse.

This led me to wonder. Is it possible that the manager of the store knows how disrespectful this woman is? A welcomer would not only have cheerfully provided me a refund, but may very likely have sympathized with me. Additionally, what better moment can there be to apprise a customer of a sale or a new item? It's not as though it's appropriate for a salesperson to randomly walk up to someone browsing the store and announce a "commercial." But it is a perfect time to express appreciation to a customer for patronizing the store. It might even make up for a negative experience someone may have had in the check-out line. A business can never make a customer feel that his business is appreciated too many times.

LET'S GO GROCERY SHOPPING

ONE PARTICULAR RETAIL food store I frequent makes a variety of freshly prepared foods, with good ingredients. One would think that the time and effort the market places in preparing the food would translate into commensurate service from those who take your order. However, among the six cashiers that

> **Customers appreciate when they are appreciated.**

work at the check-out counters, not one is a welcomer. Instead, the customer is greeted by a team of robots, whose clone-like behavior mirrors the action of characters from a science-fiction movie. It seems their entire vocabulary is made up of phrases that include, "Next in line," "Debit or credit," "Any cash back," and "Sign the screen." Their movements include scanning the items, pivoting, and placing them in awaiting bags. When one bag is full, they begin with a new bag, until finished. It's rare to hear "Hello" or "Thank you." The staff is not naturally vindictive or hostile. On the contrary, most seem quite pleasant. However, the result of the lack of communication and human interaction is a weary, impersonal atmosphere, where one's humanity is put on hold. This makes the concept of the "loyal customer" an anachronism. If one-half the staff were welcomers, the entire experience would improve profoundly.

What a Welcomer Can Accomplish with a "Hello," "a Smile" and a Few Words

- She can demonstrate that she actually noticed what the customer was purchasing.
- She can welcome the customer to the store.
- She can speak to the customer as though he were a unique individual, not one cog among an endless wheel of customers.
- She can make the customer feel relaxed, comfortable, and appreciated (something especially rewarding after a long workday).
- She can help to create a mental picture of the store as a positive place to do business.

Surprisingly, one of the new check-out folks, Annette, is a welcomer. She gives me (and her other customers) a big "Hello" and a smile. She asks how you are and does so sincerely. When I purchase an item that she herself enjoys, she mentions it, as when she remarked recently: *"I love that yogurt with the chocolate sprinkles, too!"*

Annette makes me feel special and appreciated. As the cliché goes, that's something "money can't buy." Can you imagine the store employing six welcoming cashiers? The entire neighborhood would be clamoring to shop there.

HELLO? HELLO?

A NEW TYPE of store (for those old enough to recall the era before cell phones) is the phone store. Before mobile phones, there were no such things as phone stores. Actually, there were a few here and there, but they were so rare they were novelties. One had a landline phone, received the bill each month, paid it, and that was it. With the advent of the cell phone, iPhone, and Blackberry, an army of stores has arisen, providing phone service, repair, advice, and a massive number of accessories. A few months ago, I decided to get a new phone and a new service plan. Have you ever met an individual that is constantly checking his or her phone or uses it in less than optimum situations, like while getting out of the shower, shaving, or grabbing a quick cup of coffee? Someone that tends to smack the phone down a bit too hard on the table when having lunch or multi-tasking— forgetting for a moment the phone is assembled with intricate electronics? Well, that's me.

On one particular Sunday, I arrived at the local phone store as it opened (I try to plan such endeavors when business is light). I was the first person the associate let in as he unlocked the door, and soon found myself with a choice of four service people—each seemingly alert and active behind a computer terminal. So I approached the counter. Nothing. That is, no one acknowledged I was in the store, or that I might be in the store because I wanted assistance. I would have welcomed even a nod of someone's head. I had already given up on hearing a "Hello," uttered sincerely or otherwise.

"Can anyone assist me?" I finally asked. Each of the four pivoted a head to see if a colleague was going to respond. I felt like a primary-school teacher asking the class a question and watching as the students do their best not to admit they hadn't prepared their homework.

"I will," an unenthusiastic voice uttered. This store was a branch of the telephone company I've done business with for twenty-five years! I wonder whether any of the staff could define the term "loyal customer." I definitely have my doubts. Ironically, a small sign on a distant counter displayed the message, "Please complete our two-question survey." I'm going to address the issue of survey development and implementation in another chapter. However, I don't plan to reveal what I would have written on the particular survey in the phone store, because I still believe it's important to maintain one's civility.

Not all businesses operate that way. Some understand that the "human touch" is the way to cultivate a lifelong customer. But they are getting rarer every day. Whether it is in a bank, a retail store, or a busy restaurant, keep in mind the concept of "memorable." You place your keys and wallet in a certain place so you'll have easy access to them. You remember where they

...tions that involve people need *people* to make the ...emorable. In other words, the customer experience ...: the customer with a good feeling, because the ...makes him or her feel appreciated. The solution is simple. ...ace as many welcomers in the "front-lines" as possible. If you do, and an error should arise, or a transaction seems slow, a welcomer will soothe the nerves of a patron. In fact, these flaws can be put to advantage. No one expects every check-out system to work perfectly. A welcomer can turn around a short delay with a conversation or a sincere apology, instead of what usually

occurs in these situations: three or four staff members running and shouting to find a manager to reset a cash register or check on a price.

The check-out counter should be considered the first step in the customer-retention journey, not the last process in an assembly line. Find associates that are welcomers, or at the very least, welcomer-wannabees. Make sure they understand that their behavior with customers can create and maintain long-term relationships, because of that trait every true welcomer possesses: seeing the customer as a person first and a

Wired and Dangerous

In Chip Bell's and John Patterson's best-selling book, *Wired and Dangerous: How Your Customers Have Changed and What to Do about It,* they write: "Customers are favorably attracted to organizations when they get an emotional connection. This means heart-touching encounters, filled with spirit, caring, and positive attitude. Whether in line, on-line, or face-to-face, customers recall the experience long after they've forgotten you met their need."

customer second. They notice what the customer is wearing; they remember what the customer purchased.

In so many businesses these days, retail stores are created as self-service environments. There is nothing wrong with that, if done properly. But to create a successful environment where the customer is free to browse on his or her own, you should make sure that someone in the store has the responsibility of communicating customer appreciation and that there is a welcomer that sincerely expresses the fact that he or she wants the customer back.

Let's get rid of check-out counters and replace them with reception areas, where welcomers have an opportunity to make the first and last impression. Let's instead call check-out counters, welcome-counters. Let the customer walk out of the store, thinking: "Mmm, the salesperson that took care of me made my day. She truly appreciated the fact that I purchased merchandise from *her* store, and not the store across the mall. She told me she was looking forward to seeing me again."

This sort of response doesn't come about by magic. It's simply the way most people respond to a welcomer!

In a business climate where associates don't even make eye contact with the customer, this may seem like wishful thinking. "Never happen," you might say. Well, it worked at my father's store

Typical Welcomer Comments

- "Hey that's a great scarf!"
- "You really got a great deal on that toaster oven!"
- "Is this the first time you have shopped with us?"
- "Those are my favorite potato chips."
- "I can't believe how great the weather is today."

and at thousands of stores like it. Maybe that's because hiring was based more on the attitude of the interviewee rather than his résumé. Ironically, now one can fill out applications for customer-service jobs by entering information into a computer right in the store. You won't find welcomers that way.

CAN A PERSON DO MORE THAN ONE THING AT A TIME?

WHILE WRITING THIS book, I told many friends, family members, and clients about some of its themes. Dara, a friend of my son Matt, was fascinated with the welcomer concept.

The Amazement Revolution

In Shep Hyken's book, *The Amazement Revolution: Seven Customer Service Strategies to Create an Amazing Customer (and Employee) Experience,* Shep's number four amazement strategy is: "Hire Right. We hire the right people, and we look to the right personality for the job, even before we look for technical skills." In Shep's book, he quotes Jim Bush, Vice President of American Express, on how they dramatically improved service: "By de-emphasizing the metrics, by training its people in generally unscripted soft skills, such as listening and relationship building, and by investing in new technologies that enabled customer-care professionals to make better customer-specific product and service recommendations during the call. Instead of simply trying to shorten call times, the company made the strategic decision to use the calls to improve the quality of the person-to-person connection with card members".

What got her even more enthusiastic was the fact she had found a welcomer in a dessert store within two days of having a conversation with my son about my upcoming book. When family came to town, and I was planning their itinerary, that store came to mind. Why? Not because it was written up in the Michelin Guide, but because I had recalled that Dara recommended the friendly service.

Soon all six of us walked through the front door to see what they had to offer. The first person I noticed was a young lady behind the counter. She was serving a customer. She was actually the only visible employee.

"Hi!" she said immediately. She was waiting on someone, but she still managed to smile and greet us. A few more curious pedestrians walked in moments later. "Hi!" she said to them, with the same enthusiasm. She did this several more times as the shop grew more crowded, but she still attended to the woman who was at the counter. It didn't require a major effort. Certainly no more than if she had looked up, shrugged, and shaken her head in exasperation. It just makes sense, business-wise and people-wise. We all felt welcomed and appreciated. It took no more than ten seconds for each greeting. Was it wasted time? Consider that no one acted annoyed or muttered something like, "Too crowded in here!" or "Let's find someplace else!" A welcomer first sees a customer as a person, then as a consumer. She may have just added a few regular customers to the store's business. And all it took was a few minutes. It's obvious the shop didn't cultivate a clientele through banner ads on the Internet or coupons from flyers mailed to the home. She was indicating, "You're family here. And you're just as important as anyone else." Think about it. When you're at home, sitting on your sofa, and talking on the phone, and a family member walks in—say it's your spouse or one of your children—do you ignore her as though she doesn't exist? Not if you really consider her family, rather than tolerating the fact she is. (By the way, I do realize there may be some typical teenagers that might not respond with an acknowledgment. But eventually, they'll learn.) The bottom line is that, if you enjoy what you do—in this case helping people—multi-tasking just comes naturally.

Back to our young lady. When it was our turn, she made eye contact with all of us. "How are you today? Have you been here before?" Of course, we said, "No," but it was nice that she asked. It certainly was a lot better than a robot asking, "What flavor do you want?" The question was more than just a greeting. It was a way for her to determine whether she needed to explain how the desserts were made and their ingredients.

After she had finished giving us the dessert and ringing up the transaction, I asked her for her name. She said it was Bethany. And then (and this response is just an innate one for welcomers), she asked, "What's *your* name?" I told her, and then I continued by explaining that we had chosen her store because a friend of my son had recommended it.

The weather was beautiful that day, and since the store had limited seating, my cousins and I decided to eat our desserts outside on a bench. After we were finished, I felt I needed to say goodbye, so I re-entered the store, and, although Bethany was once again waiting on a customer, she immediately noticed me. "Richard, so how did you like it?" The fact she remembered my name made me feel terrific. I felt valued and appreciated. Now, think of a different type of response. Suppose she said (and a lot of robot-types will say these sorts of things): "Did you forget something?" Does that sound cordial? First impressions are important, but last ones are too.

I realize that not every establishment can have a Bethany-type behind the counter, but you can see what a big difference it can make to customers, even if they only spend a few minutes in a store. Using some of the tools that were provided in Chapter 5 will allow your staff to act and sound more like a welcomer. It only takes one person to make you feel appreciated. Why don't businesses focus on hiring someone that will build customer loyalty? You do want a successful business, after all. In my experience, the answer lies in the fact that managers or others in a position of hiring front-line people just don't seem to readily see the connection.

To show just how important a welcomer can be for business, consider that Bethany had influenced us before we had actually *met* her. Had my son's friend not instantly recognized Bethany as a welcomer, the recommendation would never have traveled via word-of-mouth, eventually to me. Now my son's friend was tuned into identifying welcomers because he had told her of the plans for my book. But, that's fine. Acquiring this sort of knowledge; that is, the ability to recognize a welcomer is truly practical. It can definitely make a difference in your quality of life. Why would we need to be taught something that on the surface seems simply intuitive? I believe it's because we have resigned ourselves to the incivility that has crept into society in general, and sales and service, in particular. After reading this book, you will never stand in a line, pay with a credit or debit card, or be attended to by a sales or customer-service associate in a store without asking yourself, "Is this person a welcomer?" When you meet welcomers, just tell them that you appreciate the fact they

136   RICHAD R. SHAPIRO

are doing a great job. Welcomers like to make a person's day a bit nicer, but they also enjoy it when someone is considerate enough to compliment them for excellent service. It makes their day a bit better as well.

A WELCOMER HAS AT LEAST TWO SETS OF EYES

ON ANOTHER OCCASION, while I was waiting on line to purchase an item at a drugstore, the customer ahead of me had just picked up some medication that needed to be kept refrigerated. She asked the store associate if it would be okay to leave the medicine in her car for a half hour while she went on some errands. The associate admitted she wasn't an expert on the matter, but suggested that the customer simply let her keep it refrigerated in the pharmacy until she returned. That in itself demonstrated care and concern. What was especially welcoming was that she managed to let me know that she'd be right back and would assist me in a minute or so. This made me feel I was important, and that I was not dealing with a robot (who can only communicate with one person at a time). Why can't everyone do this? Is it so difficult to raise your head and say, "Hi," to the next person in line? It makes sense, it puts everyone at ease, and it's such a simple thing to do.

I CAN'T WATCH A GAME WITHOUT MY HOT DOG AND FRIES

I LOVE BASEBALL. My behavior at a ballgame is a textbook example of Pavlov's theory on conditioning. I *must* have my two ballpark franks and a large order of fries whenever I'm there.

Now, I eat healthfully the rest of the time, but when I'm enjoying two Major League teams competing against one another, health is not on my mind.

Because I *do* go to many games, I can tell you that the vast majority of folks at the snack food counters are totally robotic. They barely say "Hello", they don't engage the customers, and lots of them barely say "Thank you." However, even at the new stadium my team plays in, I found a welcomer—you'd figure a new venue means newly hired staff, which in turn means none of that old-fashioned friendly service. Well, Lois destroyed that stereotype immediately. I had arrived early, and luckily there wasn't a queue of hungry fans behind me. I was about to announce my requisite order (two franks and a side of fries), when the counter person greeted me with a big smile on her face.

"How can I help you today?" Before I responded she added, "First time at the new stadium?"

She made an immediate connection. Feeling welcomed and appreciated, I let down my guard and asked *her* a few questions. I also told her that it seemed like she loved her job.

"I better love it!" she said. "I've worked here over thirty-five years."

"How do you like the new stadium?" I asked.

She wasn't about to give me thirty-five years of her stadium wisdom, but she did mention that, while the new stadium was equipped with state-of-the-art *everything*, she missed seeing the players "up close," since, in the old stadium, the athletes came through the same doors as the stadium staff, providing her (and other staff members) a connection to the players. That connection was so strong, in fact, that *her* parents were best friends with the parents of one of the star players. Another customer stepped up, and it was time for me to depart.

"Honey, have a *great* day and enjoy the game." Lois was a natural welcomer. She was engaging; she was interested in people; she loved her job; and she knew her primary role was taking care of customers. Even the way she ended our conversation so she could take care of the next customer was done smoothly and effortlessly.

"Two franks and an order of fries, please," I heard the next customer order as I walked back to my seat—a big smile on my face!

In many cases, the associates at your company's check-out counters are the most significant folks that have the potential to increase business and, by definition, business revenue. Welcomers don't just provide excellent customer service; welcomers create a bond that can *rarely be broken.* Customers who meet welcomers want to return. They are looking for that sincere "Hello" and that genuineness that the welcomer displays. They are happy when they spot the welcomer that helped them last week or the week before. Perhaps more important, they look forward to seeing the welcomer again the following week. All these benefits accruing between the time *your* customer gets in line until *your* customer exits *your* place of business? Absolutely! Absolutely, that is, if *you* and *your associates* treat *your* customers as PEOPLE!

The Loyalty Journey

The check-out experience should start the "loyalty journey." It should be a place where initial and lasting impressions are made, and in a way that the customer is made to feel like a person first, and a consumer second.

POWER POINTS WORTH REPEATING

- In many businesses, the check-out line is potentially the only opportunity for an associate to create a customer relationship, but more and more frequently, businesses are ignoring this opportunity.
- For a retail store, particularly large ones, the return counter is the perfect place to engage a customer, especially if the customer had a complaint about a product.
- Customers appreciate when they are appreciated.
- If you have created a successful environment where the customer is free to browse on his or her own, you should make sure that someone in the store has the responsibility for communicating customer appreciation.
- The check-out experience should be the start of the "loyalty journey." It should be a place where initial and lasting impressions are made, and in a way that the customer is made to feel like a person first, and a consumer second.

7

The Great Unknown: Placing a Call

HOW DO YOUR customers feel when they call your business? Many managers don't know whether their customers feel satisfied with their phone service and often don't take sufficient time to find out. That's because they don't understand how important it is when a *potential* or *first time* customer calls. *It's not enough to simply answer the caller's questions.* Consider it an opportunity to initiate or build upon customer retention. If you haven't looked into the effectiveness of the telephone component of your sales or customer service department, there's a very strong possibility that, by the time you've made the decision to recruit welcomers, you may have already lost business. In fact, if you are still skeptical about the value of welcomers you may have lost a customer by the time you've finished reading this page!

Tone of voice and attitude mean a lot to your callers. If an associate that answers the call doesn't make that personal connection, you've missed a terrific opportunity to make a connection, and chances are you will miss out on business as well. Of course, providing accurate, factual information is important, but the way it's *expressed* is what ultimately counts. To the customer making the call, the associate's tone of voice *is* the company.

A welcomer that works in telephone customer service or sales doesn't see his or her job as answering the phone. Welcomers view the experience as a chance to develop a relationship. It's simply part of their nature. Because they think and feel this way,

---

How a Welcomer Might Answer a Call with a Simple Question

CALLER: Hi, I wanted to know what hours your store is open.

WELCOMER: Hi. My name is Jen, and I can help you with that. Do you mind giving me your name?

CALLER: It's Barbara Jones.

WELCOMER: Ms. Jones, I hope your day is going well. To answer your question, we are open from 9:00 a.m. to 9:00 p.m. during the week and from 11:00 a.m. to 9:00 p.m. on Saturdays and Sundays. When were you thinking of coming in?

CALLER: My husband generally has free time on Sundays, so probably this Sunday afternoon.

WELCOMER: Have you ever been to our store before?

CALLER: No.

WELCOMER: Sometimes people get a bit confused with the directions to our store, since we're located in the rear of the

they are going to engage whomever they have on the line.

Businesses must understand that, the more automated our society becomes, the more important conversations with their customers are. Any conversation can either build or threaten the relationship. Employing welcomers will almost ensure that conversations with potential and existing customers will create or maintain loyalty. A welcomer is automatically going to think of your customers as people first and consumers second. They are naturally engaging, and your customers will want to engage with them. They will make someone that is having a bad day

---

mall. Just follow the sign at the entrance of the mall all the way to the end. The best place to park is just to the right of our entrance. Then just walk in, pass through the women's shoe department, and you'll see the men's clothing department on the left-hand side. Did you have anything specific in mind?

CALLER: My husband is starting a new job and is looking for some nice casual business clothing.

WELCOMER: We have a great selection of fall clothing apparel, and I know that our associate James will be working that shift on Sunday afternoon. I'll let him know that you'll be in with your husband. James is great at helping our customers find what they're looking for. What's your husband's name?

CALLER: Rich.

WELCOMER: Ms. Jones, have a great day! Once again, my name is Jen. I'm going to give you my direct line. Please call back if you have any problems getting here or with any other questions you might think of.

feel better. They will treat the person like a friend. If you have a physical place of business, after speaking to a welcomer over the phone, consumers will look forward to meeting them in person.

A welcomer is going to actually have a conversation with the caller, not just answer his or her direct question. I know what you may be thinking if you own or operate a busy retail store. You don't have enough people on staff to be on the phone for three to five minutes per customer. You might be concerned you'd have to hire another part-time person just to handle inquiries. If you do think this way, you're not alone. However, it's not good business. Before the modern malls, the self-service websites, and the automated voice response systems, do you think a storeowner or an assistant announced the store hours and simply hung up? When the store was in the neighborhood, the person answering the phone sounded and acted neighborly. In fact, he or she probably *was* a neighbor, a friend, or a friend of a friend, or someone who just moved in from another town. Chances were that the owner lived nearby, and there was a good likelihood his

How a Robot-Acting Person Might Answer a Call with a Simple Question

CALLER: Hi, I wanted to know what hours your store was open.

ROBOT: From 9:00 a.m. to 9:00 p.m. during the week, and 11:00 a.m. to 9:00 p.m. on weekends.

CALLER: So you're open on Saturday and Sunday?

ROBOT: Yes, I mentioned weekends. That includes Saturday and Sunday.

kids went to the same school as yours did. The father of my best friend in elementary school owned a floor-covering business. When my family would shop for new carpet, we knew we'd be treated in a friendly, personable way.

Companies need to realize that having a telephone conversation provides a business with an opportunity to create a relationship. This generates a positive image in the mind of a potential customer. It indicates that your company will treat him or her as a person, should he or she *become* a customer. You've made the person on the other end of the phone feel important, appreciated, and valued. Think about it this way: no one likes to be taken for granted, and no one wants a company to take his or her business for granted. The customer, after all, is making an investment with his money when doing business. If your own financial advisor took your investments for granted, would that create confidence? I doubt it.

If a potential customer is responded to by a robot when making a casual inquiry, just think what is going through his or her mind. It's probably something like, "Boy, I'll be dealing with this organization quite a bit over the next year or so. Do I really want to feel as though it's a chore to communicate with them?"

The reason for apprehension about calling is that the associate or representative is acting robotically, or worse, may sound as if the inquiry is an *inconvenience* or *chore*.

Companies that use a quick-responding automated menu along the lines of "Press 1 for directions, Press 2 for hours, and Press 3 for general information," are missing the point. When someone calls your place of business—whether it's a restaurant, retail store, or beauty salon, it's an opportunity for revenue building. An electronics business wouldn't thoughtlessly load, unpack, or ship electronic merchandise. Why wouldn't that identical company treat its greatest assets, their customers, with the same respect?

HEY I'M A NEW CUSTOMER!
....

A FEW MONTHS ago, our company's health-care provider was taken over by another organization. The new company sent an impressive, upscale marketing brochure that touted the new enterprise. The rates (to my surprise) were actually a bit lower than what I had been paying for similar coverage, so it seemed appropriate to sign up with the new entity, starting on the date of our next renewal.

About two weeks after I received the eye-catching benefits brochure, someone from the new company left me a voice mail message indicating that I should call their transition team to see what questions I might have. Besides the fact that the caller who left the voice mail message wasn't courteous enough to say he'd call back at a more convenient time, his tone of voice wasn't very welcoming. It sounded as though he was simply going through a list of new clients, and I was just another anonymous name somewhere on his list. Nevertheless, I placed a call to the contact number the next day.

I called with the expectation that I was going to speak to a member of the "transition team." One would assume they would provide any technical information I'd need, since at that point I was a new or prospective customer. Common sense would tell you that it was particularly important for this group to consist of welcomers. Unfortunately, for me and the company, it was not.

My call was answered by a woman whose first inquiry was to ask me why I was calling. When I told her about the message I had received, she curtly responded, "What's your plan number?" She didn't even give me a hint of where her office or her headquarters was located. She didn't say, "I will be happy to help you." To be frank, she made me feel as though I were a moron for calling and someone that was wasting her time. After I finally reviewed the high-impact promotional packet, I gave her the plan number.

She then told me to complete the acknowledgment form before the renewal date, then mail, e-mail, or fax the form to her. That was the end of our so-called conversation. Besides her rude tone of voice, she was working on the assumption that I, a new or a potential customer, would know her e-mail address or fax number by heart. Does that indicate appreciation? If anything, it indicated that I should appreciate *her*. Doesn't this company understand that, if it asks that I call their transition department, I should be especially welcomed as a new customer? Don't they understand that I haven't decided for sure if I would be signing up with them? Here was a situation that would have been greatly benefitted by a team of welcomers.

New Customers at Risk

According to the research conducted by The Center For Client Retention, the percentage of attrition for new customers is twice as high as for long-term customers. This research reinforces the premise that new customers are more vulnerable to competition and also implies the value of building a strong relationship early in the customer's life cycle.

How a Welcomer Would Welcome a New Customer

WELCOMER: Hi, this is Mary, you have reached the transition team for ABC Company, and how can I help you?

CALLER: Someone left a message for me to call your department.

WELCOMER: I'm so glad you called. I would be happy to help you. Do you mind if I just ask you a few questions?

CALLER: Sure. Go ahead.

WELCOMER: What's your name, please?

CALLER: Richard Shapiro

WELCOMER: Hi, Mr. Shapiro, how are you doing today? I see that you are calling from New Jersey. I actually grew up in New Jersey, but in Southern New Jersey, not where your office is located. But I love the state.

CALLER: Where do you live now?

WELCOMER: In Wisconsin. I love it here too. The weather is a bit colder, but the people are so warm and friendly. Mr. Shapiro, you know that our company took over the plans from your former provider, and we would welcome the opportunity to have your company as one of our new customers. We have excellent service and we definitely appreciate our customers. We realize that providing healthcare coverage to your associates is an extremely important benefit, and we want to make sure that you understand all of the paperwork so that you can complete the forms and get them back to us before the due dates. How does that sound?

CALLER: That would definitely be helpful.

WELCOMER: Of course, we understand that you get a tremendous amount of mail and e-mail these days, and we want to make sure that you do not overlook what we sent you. Do you have a minute to go through the packet with me, so I can make sure you understand which part of the paperwork has to be completed? It is actually pretty simple.

CALLER: Yes, that would be great.

WELCOMER: Now the first thing I need to do is look up your company's records, but I need your plan number. Do you have your packet available so I can easily tell you how to find it?

CALLER: Sure. It's right in front of me.

WELCOMER: There are two sheets of paper that are printed on regular copy paper. On the top right-hand corner next to your company's name and address, there should be a number that starts with the letters BN. Do you see that?

CALLER: Yes.

WELCOMER: Great . . . [The welcomer then explains what I need to read and where I need to sign to enroll in the plan.]

WELCOMER: Okay Mr. Shapiro we're all set. By the way, how is the weather in New Jersey today? I still have some relatives there, and I heard that there was a big snowstorm on the way.

CALLER: It's actually beautiful here now. I've been too busy to listen to the forecast. I had better check.

WELCOMER: Mr. Shapiro it's been a pleasure speaking with you today, and we look forward to having your business as one of our newest clients. If it does snow, please be careful driving. Is there anything else I can help you with today?

CALLER: No. Thanks so much for your assistance. I really appreciate it.

WELCOMER: That's what we are here for. Have a great day.

I hope you can see the difference a welcomer can make. After all, they are the Doctors of First and Lasting Impressions. And if I choose to use this particular company as my benefits provider, I know I'll be speaking to them again, but I won't dread it. In fact, I may enjoy it!

MAKING A RESERVATION: MISSED OPPORTUNITIES

IT'S ALWAYS AMAZING to me that restaurants fail to use a request for a reservation as an opportunity to create loyalty and extend appreciation. It is commonly known that the restaurant industry experiences a higher rate of failure than nearly any other. There are many reasons for this, including start-up costs, keeping the business modernized and up-to-date, the long hours necessary to stay open, unpredictable food costs, and, of course, labor. Like many competitive businesses, a restaurant often is judged by the most recent meal a customer had there. In particular, I'd think restaurant owners would keep their eyes open for opportunities to build relationships with their customers and potential customers. I can't guarantee, if a restaurant has a welcomer, that simply handling reservations well and employing friendly people at the host/hostess station will assure success, but they certainly are key components. When you contact a restaurant to make a reservation, the person answering the phone all too often sounds as though she is doing you a favor. Of course, she jots down your name, but having your name in front of her, why not use it during the conversation? You're rarely asked if you have eaten there before, or whether you'd like to hear the specials of the day, or if you need driving directions or parking information.

If you happen to be the owner of a restaurant or chain of restaurants, here is my advice to you. If you have only one welcomer, assign that person to taking phone reservations. It's one of the most important components of maintaining a successful business. A welcomer is going to make a great first impression. A welcomer doesn't perceive a customer as someone who pays the bill and leaves a tip. A welcomer treats the caller as a person, and automatically gives the caller a big, "Hello, how are you today?" If the caller is a "regular," the welcomer will probably remember the caller, recall how often he or she dines there, and even a favorite table. Addtionally, sometimes when a person makes a reservation, it might be for a restaurant that has been recommended to them,

A Welcomer Leaving a Voice Mail Message

"Hi, Ms. Jones, I hope you are having a great day. This is Cindy from Amy's restaurant. We are so happy that you made a reservation through our online service and are looking forward to having you visit tomorrow evening. If you could do me a favor and just call back to reconfirm, we would really appreciate it. It helps us provide better service to all of our customers. The number is 555-555-2122. Once again, that number is 555-555-2122. I will be here until 10:00 o'clock this evening and would love to hear from you. And if this the first time you are eating here, we know that you will thoroughly enjoy your experience."

but which they'll be sampling for the first time. A welcomer can help turn a first-time customer into a long-term one before they have even dined there.

I understand that more restaurants are using online reservation systems, and these can be user-friendly and convenient. Many restaurants employing them also place a call to reconfirm that the party is still planning to come. Once again, a welcomer should be making those calls, especially when the initial message is left on voice mail. Yes, even a return call from the restaurant left as voice mail can make the customer feel good.

Sometimes people make two separate reservations at two different restaurants—deciding at the last minute which one they will honor. I can guarantee that a message left by a welcomer will significantly increase the likelihood that the customer will end up at your place instead of your competitor's.

I THOUGHT YOU SAID I WAS A VALUED CUSTOMER

I'M FASCINATED WHEN listening to those automated messages that a caller is forced to hear while waiting to speak to a representative, or when the representative places the caller on hold to look something up. A month ago, I was calling my cable provider, and the system needed to verify that the telephone number I was using was linked to my account. After I confirmed that it was, they announced that I was a valued customer and that they appreciated my business. I thought that was a nice touch, albeit an automated one. I had placed the call to my cable company because I decided to drop some of the services I was paying for, but never used. I was particularly motivated since the company had just raised its rates.

When I reached a representative and explained the reason for my call, she was efficient enough, but robotic in tone. She proceeded to cancel the services I didn't want, but then informed me I'd be paying a five-dollar fee for making the change. Consider that my new lower bill made my cable service fees about $1,500.00 a year. I have been a customer for the last ten years.

"The recording said I was a valued customer. If I am so valued, why would you charge me five dollars to adjust my account," I asked.

Evidently, she couldn't appreciate the logic behind my inquiry. She simply and robotically repeated the company policy. I asked her my question a second time. At that point she agreed to waive the fee, but not before she advised me that this was a one-time only courtesy. Does it require such forethought to realize that a customer only contacts a cable company once or twice a year (at most), so it presents a rare opportunity for it to communicate their appreciation of my long-term commitment? Instead, they used my call to increase their revenues over the short term.

GETTING ME AS A LIFETIME CUSTOMER WITHOUT A PURCHASE

DURING THIS PAST year, I had a business trip to San Francisco, which is a six-hour flight from the East Coast. My laptop computer has a battery life of about 3 1/2 hours, and I had quite a bit of work to do. I had heard that there was a store in my neighborhood that carried external battery packs for my laptop and was known for great service, so I called to inquire about purchasing one.

The sales representative that took my call was a definite welcomer. She immediately identified herself by name and asked how she might help me. I asked for some basic information about the store: its hours of operation, and how long a wait I could expect if I dropped by. Louise was terrific. She asked, "How are you?" before even asking why I was calling. She was upbeat and sounded truly glad to talk to me. When she found out that I needed the extended battery for one or two business trips, she checked to see whether the item was in stock. But before asking whether she should put it aside for me, she explained airlines had started to install electrical outlets on their newer planes. I should find out if my flight featured them and I wouldn't need to buy a pricey accessory I'd only use once or twice. I thanked Louise profusely for this information. However, Louise thought it was simply the proper thing to do. She told me if I still needed the part that the store would have it, and that I should ask for her personally if decided to come by.

Louise was right. My plane *was* equipped with an outlet. I will never forget Louise, and how helpful she was. I was not even a customer, but she made me feel important, appreciated, and valued. She assisted me in the same way any of us would help out a family member or close friend. I'm making sure to tell my friends and colleagues about my experience, so they know whom to call and whom to do business with in the future.

Yes, it's the "Louises" of the world that can start customers on their retention journeys. Don't miss these opportunities. Try calling your company to ask for directions, make a reservation, or ask just a simple question and see whether, if you were a "real" customer, the phone encounter would have positively affected your loyalty. Millions of companies miss millions of opportunities to demonstrate customer appreciation when their phone rings.

POWER POINTS WORTH REPEATING

- Many companies don't understand how important it is when a *potential* or *first time* customer calls. *It's not enough to simply answer the caller's questions.*
- To the customer making the call, the associate's tone of voice *is* the company.
- Businesses need to understand that the more automated our society becomes, the more important a conversation with their customers is.
- In many industries, the attrition rate for new customers is twice as high as for long-term customers, reinforcing the value of building a strong customer relationship early in the customer's life cycle.
- Companies need to realize that having a telephone conversation provides a business with an opportunity to create a relationship.

8

Online Shopping: Who's Behind the Curtain?

EVERYONE HAS PROBABLY seen the movie *The Wizard of Oz*, if not once, then numerous times. If you recall, we discover that the Wizard is just an average man that hid behind a curtain. He had no magical powers at all. What does this non-magical wizard have to do with customer service? When consumers are searching sites to purchase something they need or want for the first time, they never really know what kind of service they will receive. What if they need to return something? What are the shipping policies? What if I have a question about one of the items; how long will it take for someone to get back to me? Will he be friendly or robotic? Basically, the computer screen is like the curtain from *The Wizard of Oz*. When you are dealing with an e-commerce site for the first time, you really don't know whether the company employs associates like those at Zappos, who understands and appreciates customers, or like those at an organization that feels that it's sufficient to staff its departments with robots, indifferent, or hostiles.

It is estimated that online shopping has risen to over 250 billion dollars in just a few years. It's great for a company to know that more and more of its business can be generated online, because there are many cost advantages to selling products and services via the Web, rather than through the older, conventional ways of doing business. But on the flip side, anyone can start selling merchandise online with almost no initial investment. This is a big transformation from the past, when firms needed to have the capital to invest in purchasing or leasing space and everything that goes into maintaining a brick and mortar store. So, what does that mean for business? It's clear that competition is going to be substantially greater each year. One way to differentiate your business from everyone else's is by offering lower costs, but this strategy can eventually result in a company going out of business. That business could very well be yours. The alternative way to remain competitive is to provide the best service and support. If you own or manage a company that offers online shopping and have welcomers that innately understand how to treat customers as people first and consumers second, you will surely have a head start. The reason welcomers treat consumers that way is because welcomers *think* of customers that way. It just comes naturally to them.

Companies have to realize that when consumers are shopping online—from the moment they select their items until they pay for them through the "check-out" function, a great deal of human emotion is connected with navigating a website and selecting those clicks. A computer is a robot, but consumers are not. When consumers are making their online choices, besides the financial investment, they are thinking about a number of things that reflect their emotional investment as well: "Am I making the right choice?" "Is my friend, Sue, going to like what I purchased?" "Can I really afford this item?" "Will it be delivered on time?" "Would I have been better off purchasing this item in a store where I can actually see it?" "Did I select the right size, and if I didn't, will they honor the return policy?" "How nice will I look in it?" "Will my friends notice?" There's a lot more involved than simply making a left-click with your mouse.

When consumers purchase products or services, particularly for the first time, they don't know who is behind that electronic curtain. Let's face it. A website is simply an electronic brochure and order form that responds robotically with every click a consumer makes. What a real life person wants is the security of knowing there is another real, live person behind that website that will treat him or her like a person first, and then a consumer.

One of the principal assumptions of this book is that many interactions with a merchant are just one-time events, unless a company can make a connection with a consumer as soon as he or she becomes a customer. By its nature, electronic communication is impersonal. But a business that employs electronic communication need not treat customers impersonally. Companies need to understand that making a customer feel welcomed, important, and appreciated is equally important, if not more so, when the communication is designed for an electronic, self-service environment.

Shopping online elicits the same emotions as buying in a store, perhaps even stronger ones. When emotions are involved, consumers frequently feel the need to interact with another person. Many companies are taking heed of this fact, and are realizing that communication is not only the key to turning a profit, it is central to making a business flourish.

Two young men in their twenties recently started up a company that allows its customers to create customized men's shirts for a very reasonable price. In addition, the site is quite cool and consumer friendly. It's automated so that the buyer creates his or her own unique shirt. But the website also makes it easy to get live help. The company was profiled in the May 15, 2010, edition of *The New York Times,* in an article entitled, "Putting Customers in Charge of Design." Here is an excerpt that illustrates that these entrepreneurs understand the importance of welcoming customers for business development and growth: One goal was to communicate directly with customers: "The website commands: "Call us. We like to talk."

Depending on the time of day, the owner answers the calls himself. When he is awake, he also activates a feature that sends instant messages to customers who have been on the site for more than 90 seconds.

Need help? He asks. For several hours a day, he and his partners chat with customers about what they like and don't like on the site.

The feedback has led to several site revamps and—I can't resist—alterations. The company is on its third home page in six months, and the partners say they tweak the site every day.

By communicating directly with customers, this company has the opportunity to make the customer feel welcomed, important, and appreciated.

What these two young entrepreneurs understand is that their consumers want to know that there are people behind the electronic curtain and not robots. Doesn't that make sense? What *doesn't* make sense is when companies make it virtually impossible to send an e-mail, or for heaven's sake, allow a customer or prospective customer to speak to a live person over the phone.

DON'T REPLY TO THIS E-MAIL

I LOVE THOSE e-mails that inform you that your account will automatically be renewed, and in large letters, right in the body of the e-mail is the phrase, "Do not respond to this e-mail."

I recently tried to cancel an annually-renewed subscription for a malware software package, because I no longer used the computer in which I had it installed. I tried to reach numerous departments of the software company to inform them not to charge my card. In return, I received four or five e-mails informing me that I "reached the wrong department." E-mails to their tech support, renewal support, and customer support saying "I NO LONGER HAVE THE COMPUTER. PLEASE CANCEL MY SUBCRIPTION!" were typed and sent in vain. If this isn't a totally robotic way of treating customers, I don't know what is. I became so frustrated and infuriated that I finally contacted my credit card company to give them a heads-up. Will I ever do business with this company again? Will I ever recommend them? No way!

Companies need to realize that they should provide a means for human interaction, and when appropriate, human intervention. These options make customers feel comfortable and instill confidence in situations where they want to reconfirm something regarding a transaction or ask a question about a product. They are simply seeking a prompt, informed, and *sincerely concerned* response. I've mentioned in an earlier chapter that the check-out counter in a brick and mortar store needs to be designed so that it can be the start of the consumer's retention journey. Companies that use the Web to sell their wares need to understand that the retention journey starts with my first click.

With more products and more complex products on the market, people have more and more questions. Some companies have on-line chat capabilities; others have "Contact Us" pages, although the latter are sometimes difficult to find. Others have a link to Frequently Asked Questions or FAQs. Unfortunately, if your question is not one of the frequent ones, you have no way of having *your* question answered. There's usually an option for e-mailing a company, should a consumer have an inquiry, but it's imperative that your company have welcomers who respond to those e-mails. Even the emotional tone of an e-mail differs if it's written by a robot, rather than a welcomer. Make sure the associates that respond to consumers (many who are using your site for the first time), have the traits of a welcomer or are taught to use some of the tools in the welcomer-wannabees tool kit.

Since our company specializes in conducting consumer satisfaction and loyalty research, people often ask me whether it's true that an electronic response is capable of making a connection. The answer is that an e-mail response *absolutely* can create a relationship if written by a caring person. While conducting research for my book, I e-mailed many companies and used plenty of on-line websites. With some of the e-mails, I adopted the role of a mystery shopper and posed as a typical consumer.

In one scenario, I explained that I was a grandfather looking to use the site to purchase a holiday gift for one of my grandsons, and needed some assistance. I e-mailed ten different companies to see how they would respond. Here is what I found. Of the ten companies, one e-mailed me back within a half-hour. The response was well-worded. Four companies sent an auto response, explaining that they had received my e-mail and would respond within two days. One of the four actually did. In addition, three informed me that my e-mail query was sent to an address that was no longer valid. Of course, I wondered why it was still listed on their site. Two never replied at all.

The company that responded within thirty minutes won the consumer response prize. It also happened to be one of the largest and most successful teenage apparel retailers. The e-mail was detailed and professional. It provided all the information a grandparent would need or want to know. It was a perfect example of a welcoming response.

That response made me feel that my business would be appreciated. They clearly understood that I might not be comfortable ordering online, so they offered to help me with the ordering process over the phone. They made me feel that I contacted the

Specific Phrases that Are Very Welcoming

- "*Thanks* for e-mailing us about exploring our site."
- "We *would love to help* you find the perfect gift for your grandson."
- "*If you would like, you can call in* and place your order over the phone."
- "One of our brand representatives *will be able to walk you through* the ordering process and answer any questions you may have."
- "We *hope you find the perfect gift* for your grandson."

right place. They understood that I wanted to make my grandson happy. They took into account my specific inquiry, and it's clear that it wasn't a canned response.

PURCHASING SHOES FOR MY GRANDSON

FOR ANOTHER SCENARIO, I wrote that I was a grandmother who was looking to purchase a pair of shoes, and my grandson had recommended their site. This time a different online retailer—already known for outstanding service—did a great job of making me feel welcomed.

I liked the way this company handled my e-mail request for help. The representative realized that thanking the consumer's grandson up front would be important. They too provided the option of speaking to a representative over the phone. Moreover, they wished the consumer a wonderful day. Additionally, they provided

Key Meaningful Phases

- "I'd be *more than happy to assist* you with your experience today."
- "*Please tell your grandson thank you* for referring you to us."
- "If *you feel more comfortable* calling in and speaking with one of us *you are more than welcome to.*"
- "Harriett, I hope this e-mail was helpful, *if you have any further questions, please let us know.*"
- "*Have a wonderful day!*"

detailed instructions that almost anyone could follow with ease.

In both cases, the wizard behind the curtain provided magical service. Additionally, each of the e-mails was signed by a specific person, not an anonymous department. Consumers can relate to people. One was Cheryl, and the other was Gregory. Congratulations to both of these representatives for knowing how to make their customers feel welcomed, important, and appreciated.

Sample of Follow-up E-mail

Mr. Shapiro,

I want to once again thank you for e-mailing our company about purchasing a gift for your grandson. I was the representative who responded to your request. I hope that I provided you with enough information to make a decision and that you purchased the items online or by directly speaking with one of the other team members.

If you still have not purchased the item and need help, we are here for you.

I know that consumers have many choices, but I want you to know that we appreciate all of our customers and do not take any for granted.

Hope you have a great day!

Sincerely,

Gregory

Customer Support

Another suggestion I have for any company that offers online shopping is a follow-up response. Following up is something that few companies do at all and nearly no company does well. However, a welcomer would probably follow-up automatically. If a consumer e-mails a company, asking for help with a pending purchase, the company should send the consumer a follow-up e-mail. It should ask whether the customer's question was answered, or whether the item they purchased was satisfactory.

Sample E-Mail for a First-Time User of Your Company's Site

Mrs. Jones,

Since you just registered, you are probably using our site for the first time. We hope that you found the site easy to navigate, but if you had any problems, we want to hear from you. Our e-mail address is we-care@abcompany.com. Our telephone number is 201-555-3240. We are available twenty-four hours a day.

We do hope that you will be a customer of ours for many years to come, but we also understand this will not happen unless you have smooth sailing with us during your first experience.

That's what I'm here for: to make sure that your first experience is problem-free and memorable.

Sincerely,

Joe

Customer Support

ABC Company

At a minimum, the e-mail should thank them for using your website. A properly worded follow-up e-mail can go a long way to demonstrate loyalty to the consumer, and start the customer on the retention journey.

A follow-up e-mail distinguishes your company. It can demonstrate that your business cares, that you treat the customer with respect, that you appreciate him or her as a person first, and a consumer second.

Very few companies take the opportunity to thank their customers for their business. In the online environment, there are several appropriate times when the consumer can be thanked and acknowledged.

Passwords Can Be Key to Repeat Business

Registering on a site provides the company with a great opportunity to contact a consumer or a potential one, but there are other times that also provide excellent opportunities for the company to demonstrate customer appreciation. One is when consumers request new passwords. Often, when consumers ask for passwords, it indicates they haven't used your site for a while. Sending a new password via an automatic response without a follow-up e-mail is an indication to many people that you treat your customers robotically. In addition, customers appreciate the fact that you recognize that they've been long-time customers. It means they value what you have to offer, so you should show gratitude for their loyalty. Customers do not like to be taken for granted, and if they are, they may take their business elsewhere. After all, switching to your competitor is only a few clicks away.

Frequently, the first time is when they register on the site. They may have not made a purchase yet or finalized a transaction, but a sincere e-mail from a welcomer would distinguish your company as being consumer-friendly.

Companies must realize that an investment in human interaction goes hand-in-hand with a well-executed on-line site. It's often necessary to let the consumer know immediately that there's a welcomer ready to assist him or her. A welcomer understands the emotions surrounding the purchasing of an item, particularly an expensive item such as a home entertainment center, an automobile, furniture, or other items that require a sizeable investment. A welcomer provides magical service: transforming customer concern and anxiety to customer confidence.

ALMOST EVERYONE GOES ONLINE FIRST TO PURCHASE A NEW CAR

JIM, A FRIEND of mine, was recently in the market for a new car. Automobile companies have some of the most lavish and coolest sites. They often provide on-line tools to custom fit your own car online. Up until a few years ago, you would still purchase a car from a dealer showroom, where you may have known the salesperson. Now, most consumers that plan to purchase a car go online first. That makes a great deal of sense. You can see the models, find prices, learn about options, and compare models from different manufacturers.

Jim had narrowed his choice to two. The companies that offered these models had consumer-friendly and innovative websites, and both have excellent reputations in the mid-size automobile market. So Jim spent some time in designing his own car: one from each of the two on-line sites. Of course, the purchase isn't transacted online. You still need a salesperson to find out if the car is in inventory, inform you about their service department, and create the final paperwork.

The same day that he had "built" his ideal car on the two sites, he received e-mail responses from both. But the e-mails were vastly different. One manufacturer responded within an hour, but informed Jim that the salesperson at the dealership closest to him was away for a week's vacation, and would contact my friend at that time. Nearly everyone knows that, when you are ready to purchase a car, you don't want to wait a week to discuss it. The company has a terrific website, so why don't they follow through with equally terrific service? Get it? It certainly does not make sense.

The other manufacturer also sent an e-mail, but this one indicated how happy the dealership felt that Jim was interested in purchasing one of their models and that "Joseph Smith" would be contacting him by the end of that day to set up an appointment.

Joseph called as promised, and he turned out to be a true welcomer. In this case, the phone call was a critical link to the final purchase. Joseph immediately made Jim feel important, appreciated, and welcomed as a customer. When my friend arrived for his appointment, the first thing Joseph wanted to know was where Jim lived. As it turned out, they both resided in the same neighborhood, and knew many of the same people. Joseph saw my friend as a person first and consumer second. My friend Jim's experience with a promptly arranged meeting with a "real life person" was important. And he purchased the car he had designed without a hitch.

As a footnote, the other car company didn't contact Jim in a week. In fact, they never followed up at all. Is it any surprise why a company may be baffled as to why a competitor is doing well, while its own business is floundering? In politics, it's often said that, regardless of the candidate, "It's the economy, stupid." For businesses to excel they need to understand that it's the person first. Everything else is secondary.

Another area where human interaction is being replaced by on-line transactions is the banking and investment industry. You can be sure that most people will only engage in these transactions if they feel safe, and the best way to ensure this (besides the obvious requirement of a secure website) is to make users feel that there are concerned people behind the website "curtain" that will make them feel valued and appreciated. I had an experience with one such organization that did everything right.

A WELCOMING MESSAGE

OUR COMPANY OFFERS its associates a 401K plan, and since its inception, the funds have been sent to the 401K administrator through the mail. However, that company has had a campaign to convince its clients to electronically transmit their contributions through its secure website. First, I received an e-mail that introduced the specific reason for the change, and explained why it would be beneficial. The e-mail was signed by

"Jennifer," who said that she would follow up the e-mail with a telephone call.

A day or two later, Jennifer called. She clarified the new procedures, and recommended I review them to see if I had any further questions. I agreed. However, I'm a busy guy, and frankly, that was not my first priority. But Jennifer sent me a nicely worded follow-up e-mail a few days later, telling me that she was there to answer any questions that I may have. She reiterated that electronically transmitting the required information to set up an Internet account would be quite easy and that she could walk me through the entire process when I had time to speak with her. This company also got it! They integrated their electronic communication with a person that sounded like a welcomer. She made me feel that she was there to support my initial transaction and to help in any way. She understood (and the company understood) that people don't like to change, especially when life is so hectic. Having a welcomer to assist you is like having a friend that can make you feel good in rough times and even better in good ones.

I often crack a smile when I receive an electronic e-mail blast from a company that "wants me back." Frankly, it's way too late. People don't like to change, but once they have made a decision to go elsewhere, you are throwing your money away if you invest time and dollars in former customers. Make sure you express your company's appreciation at the appropriate time with *current* customers. Make sure they know that your service is magical and that in *your* company, the Wizard of Oz isn't a huckster, but a welcomer that possesses the welcomer traits.

POWER POINTS WORTH REPEATING

- By its nature, electronic communication is impersonal. But a business that employs electronic communication need not treat customers impersonally.
- Companies need to understand that they should provide a means for human interaction, and when appropriate, human intervention.
- Companies that use the Web to sell their wares need to understand that the retention journey starts with the customer's first click.
- Sending a consumer a follow-up e-mail if a purchase was not made within a short period of time is another opportunity to build a connection
- Very few companies take the opportunity to thank their customers for their business. In the on-line environment, there are several appropriate times when the consumer can be thanked and acknowledged.
- Sending a new password via an automatic response without a follow-up e-mail is an indication to many people that you treat your customers robotically

9

Why Ask Me "How Was Everything Today?" If You Don't Really Care?

I LEFT THE corporate world to start a research company, based on the premise that we could offer an important service by conducting conversations with consumers and business executives to garner their feedback on behalf of our clients. It could be as simple as getting a response from a consumer about a recent interaction, or as thorough as learning how an executive felt about a long-standing business relationship. In effect, we are offering a service to gain comprehensive feedback by engaging the customers of our clients in conversation. After nearly twenty-five years in business, it's fair to say I had a good idea that there was and is a need for this service. It is great to get an independent, objective, third-party assessment of what customers think about a company's service, but we always have explained to our clients that, though we can get the ball rolling, they have to learn how to develop a relationship that can continue to be nurtured.

We've established that welcomers are few and far between, but we also explained how there are many tools in the welcomer-wannabee's tool kit that can make a large number of robots sound more welcoming. However, it should be equally clear by now that robots make up the largest group of sales or customer service associates. What is one of the most common questions a robot is likely to ask at a check-out counter? "Do you want your card transaction to be debit or credit?" Of course, that's an appropriate question to ask, but is it sufficient? Even robotic personnel know they should say more than that, and they often do. But what happens when a robot asks a question that focuses on you as a person? Some of the most widely used (and abused) of these questions include, "How was everything today?" or "Did you find what you need?" or "How are you doing?" When such inquiries (or similar ones) are posed by anyone but a welcomer, many times they sound robotic and rarely solicit anything more than a one-word answer like "Fine" or "Yes" or "Good." That's because, other than welcomers, most service providers don't act or sound like they generally care. If consumers sense that the person inquiring doesn't want to hear the answer, they respond with one or two words. Moreover, that response isn't likely to reflect the truth. Why share how you're truly feeling with someone that has no emotional connection with you and isn't interested in creating one?

Since welcomers see the consumer as a person first and a customer second, it means that when you reach the check-out counter, they are more interested in your state of mind than your method of payment. Welcomers also have "emotional radar." They can immediately sense your general disposition from your expression, even if they've never met you before. They also notice what you purchase and comment on it if appropriate. "That's a great shirt. If we had one in my size, I would have bought it for myself," a welcomer might say.

If the customer looks sad or doesn't smile, a welcomer won't *ask* how he is feeling or how she is feeling. He will reach out and say something like, "It looks as if you are having rough day" or "Is everything okay?" A welcomer can connect almost immediately by engaging with the customer, not by asking her a robotic question or two.

Do you remember Javier from the chapter devoted to welcomers? He said his job at the deli counter was to "put a smile on someone's heart." A welcomer knows how to do that: by engaging the person in a conversation and by connecting emotionally. For a welcomer, there is *no* secret formula. It's something they just *know* is the right thing to do.

I would say that two of the industries where associates consistently ask, "How was everything today?" or "How was your experience with us?" are restaurant and hotel businesses. Frankly, it doesn't matter whether you had a great experience at a restaurant or a bad stay at a hotel, most of the time you just respond with a curt "fine." Most consumers will *say* "fine" or "OK" because they have no desire to engage with someone who doesn't care about the answer. Now, you might think, "Well, I'm not going to tell someone that my pet had to be put away yesterday, that my best friend is in the hospital, or that I'm excited because my daughter is getting married this weekend, or sad because my only son just left for college, and I miss him terribly."

That's typically true. But if you're in the presence of a welcomer, he or she will sense that something is either wrong or right, and engage you. Without even being aware of opening up, you will soon realize that you told someone that was previously a stranger something that's personal. After just one experience of meeting a welcomer, a customer returning to that hotel or restaurant will actively look for the person with that unique trait. Once a consumer discovers your business has that rare individual who is a welcomer, he will get the "welcomer bug," not simply because he was treated well, but because he wants to get to know the Doctor of First Impressions even better.

A WELCOMER CAN BE THE LOYALTY GLUE

LES, A NEIGHBOR of mine, explained that when he goes to his neighborhood supermarket, he always waits in line for one particular cashier. I asked him why he would do that, when another line might in fact be shorter. When he described this cashier, I knew he was talking about a welcomer. A welcomer has a quality that you can immediately identify, even when a third party is describing it.

Les said, "Mary's register always has five or six people in line, while the other cashiers might have just one or two."

I asked Les why Mary's line was always more crowded than the others. Les gave me a glance, smiled, and said, "Mary really *wants* to know how you're doing. Not only that, but I want to really know how *Mary* is doing!"

Well, I'm not an attorney, but I think that Les would be a terrific expert witness if I wanted to prove my point about welcomers in a court of law.

Les also revealed another principle of why welcomers are great for business. Welcomers create a situation that becomes a two-way connection. If you own any business with multiple check-out lines, and one line is regularly longer than the others (I'm assuming it's not because of incompetence), pay attention! You probably have a Doctor of First Impressions in your midst. A welcomer is the loyalty glue that keeps customers coming back and can start the retention journey in an instant. Or think of a welcomer as a magnet that pulls your customer to your establishment instead of to your competitor's.

One of the most common questions I get is what to do about robotic-acting service and salespeople that care about what

Welcomers Are Not Just for Shopping

In New York, it's an understatement to say there are many stores. However, why do I only shop in one store for most of my clothing? It's because of Laureta. If Laureta weren't a salesperson in this store, I probably wouldn't shop there at all. However, not only will I pay the store a visit to buy a sweater or shirt, I'll simply stop in when I'm in the area, and say hello. Why? Every time I see Laureta, she says, "Mr. Shapiro, it is so good to see you today. How have you been?" And Laureta wants to know. She doesn't settle for a one-or two-word answer. She asks me for details, for example, she inquires how my sons are doing. Lately, she's been asking me about the progress of my book. I ask her about her kids. Laureta is like a friend. She cares. She doesn't have a robotic molecule in her.

they do, but don't have that special welcomer touch. It could be that the associate is a bit shy, or maybe isn't sure how to act, but is hesitant to admit it. I'm hoping that when a robotic-acting service provider reads this book, he or she will think and speak in a more welcoming fashion. This doesn't mean he or she will magically transform into a welcomer, but it could provide a better experience for the customers, which will pay off for the manager or executive.

CAN A WELCOMER BE LUCKY ENOUGH TO END UP WITH TWO SONS WHO ARE WELCOMERS TOO?

MY TWO SONS Michael and Matthew are in the restaurant business. Michael is general manager of a restaurant in Manhattan, and Matthew is working towards a management position at a popular restaurant in Boulder, Colorado. Both of them know the principle of the restaurant business called "touching a table." What touching a table means is introducing yourself and getting to know your guests. This can't be successfully done by just walking over and saying, "How is everything going today?" during the meal or after the check has been paid. Customers can see right through a mechanically delivered question like that. Would spending an extra thirty seconds with your customers be a waste of time in a fast-paced business? Actually, it would be the reverse. I'm sure you know the expression, "Penny-wise and pound foolish."

Let's listen into some of the questions a welcomer might use to get to know his customers better.

- "Is this the first time you are dining with us this evening?"
- "Welcome to our restaurant."
- "And what's your name?"
- "Why did you decide to dine with us this evening?"
- "What was your favorite dish?"
- "Did anyone regret selecting the item he ordered this evening?"

You may be saying to yourself, "Well, that's an entire conversation!" And you'd be right. You'd also be losing out on business if you or your staff does not engage in similar conversations with *your* customers. Michael finds out his customers' names, where they're from, how was their experience at the restaurant, and what are their plans for making a return visit. Michael uses this opportunity to learn about hundreds of people. This isn't just good for business; it's good for the spirit. Recently he found out one of his customers was his little league coach. He has met people that turned out to be friends of his high-school teachers. One diner was the owner of several well-known restaurants in town. If Michael feels it's appropriate, he might tell his customers to ask for him on their next visit, or invite them to ask for him personally over the phone if they're booking a reservation.

So what I'm saying is, if you are not a welcomer and care about your business, try to get to know your customers along the way—as people. Find out what got them there in the first place. That could be a great way to understand them as living, breathing people, not just names in a computer database.

Welcomers find out about *their* customers over time. It's imperative that businesses understand that information is the key. The more you know about a person, the better sales or customer-service experience you will deliver. And the better you know the individual as a person and not just as a customer, the greater motivation the customer will have to go out of her way to do business at your establishment, rather than your competitor's.

Having welcomers on staff is like having insurance. How many businesses would feel secure operating without property or casualty insurance, workmen's compensation, and any other insurance that is either mandated or highly recommended? Very few. So why would you not have "customer retention" insurance? Think of welcomers as another form of insurance. In their case, however, it's a policy of investment, not of expense. If

Sample Questions that Almost Any Establishment Can Use

- How did you hear about our establishment?
- Have you heard from neighbors about our store, and if so what did you hear?
- What did you need today that made you go shopping?
- Why did you make a special effort to come out in this hot weather or rain to buy something?
- Do you have a special occasion coming up?
- Have you been in the store before?
- Did you grow up in this area or someplace else?

you think the time you may need to find a welcomer is costing you money, consider that it will be time that will pay off down the road.

If you are the only restaurant downtown, or the only home building-supply store within a ten-mile radius, you might say, "I'm not worried. I'm the only game in town."

First, that's generally not the case, and second, a competitor may decide to *move* into town. Welcomers will make your customers want to come back, even with new competition. Welcomers are the magnets that draw your customers to your

How Much Is a Welcomer Worth in Terms of Dollars?

How much a welcomer is worth in dollars really depends. But it's easy to figure out if you consider your consumers' behaviors. Here's an example. Let's say you own a dry-cleaning business and your average cleaning ticket is $9.00. A typical customer brings in clothes for cleaning twice a month. That customer is worth $9.00 x 12 months x 2 times a month, which equals $216.00 a year. Many consumers, even ones that might move from one house to another, still stay in the same geographical area. Let's say one lived in an area for five years, and walked into your business when he or she first moved into the neighborhood. If we take an average estimate for those five years, then the customer is not just worth nine dollars every time he or she walks in. The customer is really worth $216.00 a year times five years, or $1,080.00. What the manager or owner of a business must consider is not the nine-dollar, bi-weekly sale, but the full five years of business.

place of business. Welcomers are always welcomers. They are Doctors of First and Lasting Impressions. They know your customers want to be considered people first, then consumers. If you've wondered why one of your associates is special, why customers ask for a particular associate when they walk into your business, consider whether the associate has those welcomer characteristics. If so, chances are you already employ a welcomer. If that's the case, my advice is to treat him as a professional. It doesn't matter what school he graduated from or how impressive his résumé might appear. Place him in front-line positions, and keep him there. And make sure that your company compensates him appropriately. As I've said, I can't make suggestions regarding what an appropriate salary or benefit package should be for a welcomer. There are many factors to consider, such as the size of your business, where you are located, what the general salary scale looks like at your company, and so on. But if you realize that a customer has the potential for a lifetime of value, a welcomer may be key to retaining him or her. Consider this. More than

Customer Retention Insurance Policy

Any business can ask itself the following two questions to determine how secure its customer base really is: Are long-term customers loyal, or are they at-risk survivors, just waiting for a better or more conveniently located establishment to open up? Are you willing to see whether your customer base is secure without welcomers on board? That's your prerogative, but I wouldn't experiment on my business that way.

ever, stores that have on-site merchandise make sure they have appropriate security measures in place to protect inventories. More important than your inventories are your customers. By ignoring the importance of welcomers, you are placing your largest asset at risk. What's that worth? You figure it out.

It's critical to any business to get good customer feedback. Customer feedback is not asking, "How is everything going today?" We know now that frequently the answers to those questions are unreliable and provide no real value. I'm not suggesting you substitute that question with a quick two-item survey either. That won't provide any additional insight. What I am recommending is that you develop a comprehensive plan to be sure to have a conversation with your customers by a staff member or a team of members that know what questions to ask, and can carry out the survey in a supportive, non-threatening environment. If that's not possible, then get an independent third party that can determine what your "at-risk customer loss" factor is.

Businesses frequently ask me "what's a good sample size"? Generally, in research that measures

Mystery Shopper Calls, Visits, E-Mails

While mystery-shopper services can be highly valuable, if a company has limited funds for studying consumers, I would not place my resources in mystery shopper research first, simply because mystery shoppers are not really your customers. I would talk directly to real customers that can relay real experiences and communicate real emotions about shopping in your establishment.

personal preference, a sample of 100 usually is sufficient to determine the outcome for the entire population within a reasonable degree of confidence. When *The Wall Street Journal* conducts presidential election polls every four years, the sample population that's surveyed is usually less than 1,000 people. Yet, over 120 million people voted in each of the past two presidential elections. It's true that polls are not accurate 100 percent of the time. Generally, when people plan to vote, their attitudes are like bouncing balls: they may change their vote several times during the pre-election period. However, if a repeat customer walks into your establishment, he or

Sample Questions to Ask One Hundred Random Customers

- Why did you select us in the first place?
- What do we do best?
- If there is one thing that we could change to make your life and your family's life a bit easier, what would that be?
- Have you ever used a competitor of ours?
- If so, how did their service and support compare to ours?
- When you call for an appointment, how do our people sound?
- Do the associates that answer our phones do so right away or do you have to wait a while before making your inquiry?
- Do they make you feel welcomed?
- Do we ever say or do anything that makes you feel as though we value your business?
- If a new neighbor moved next door to you and asked you for a recommendation, what would you say about us?

she most likely has an opinion of your business. In your role as a business owner or manager, not knowing your "at risk customer loss" factor is being negligent in your responsibilities, especially since it's not difficult to find out.

If a hundred of your regular customers respond to many of the sample questions I have provided, you will be able to determine your "customer survivor percentage" and "at risk retention ratio." If you discover from the answers that you have some welcomers on board, make sure you thank them and ensure that they stay in your employ. If you find you have customers that are only doing business with you because of the convenience, eventually you will have a problem. You need not rush and conduct these customer interviews right away. Just make sure that you have planned the process to yield accurate results. Timing is not as critical as the actual process.

If you own or manage a typical retail establishment, where potential customers walk in and walk out without making a purchase, or if you notice that only some do business, you need to find out why. You need to speak to a hundred customers. I would suggest that, if you have already recognized a Doctor of First Impressions on your staff, that you have him or her ask consumers as they are leaving, "Would you be kind enough to sit down briefly and talk about your experience with another associate before you leave?"

I'd be sure to include people that didn't purchase anything. They are just as important as those that did. My cousin Sam calls those folks "wanderers." They are people that came into your establishment for a specific reason, but walked out for any number of reasons. To ignore these "wanderers" is a business

Sample Questions to Ask Customers Who Purchased and Those Who May Have Not

- Is this the first time you're in the store?
- What was the initial reason you had for stopping in?
- Are you a regular customer?
- What do you like best about coming to the store?
- What is the one thing that the store could change that would make your shopping experience easier?
- Who assisted you at the store?
- Compared to staff at other retail stores, how helpful was the person (or persons)?
- If you're a regular customer, what makes you return?
- I see you made a purchase today. Is there anything in particular that would encourage you to shop here again?
- I see you didn't purchase anything today. What were you initially looking for?
- I see you didn't buy anything today. Was that because the people did not seem to be knowledgeable? Was the price more than what you intended to spend? (Here you could ask additional follow-up questions depending on your type of inventory or service).
- If you were the owner of this store or this chain, what suggestions would you have to improve service or brand selection?
- Did you find anyone at the store that truly made you feel appreciated or welcomed, the way a friend or neighbor might?
- If a friend of yours asked, "How was your visit to MyRetailStore?" what would you tell him or her about your experience?

mistake. I know what you may be thinking: "Who is going to take the time to sit down for five or ten minutes to tell me about her experience in this busy world?

So as not to place pressure on anyone, I'd simply ask the people that are doing the survey to first ask, "Could you help me out, please?" Most people want to help, especially when someone requests it. I'd then have the interviewer mention that your business is conducting important customer research.

I can guarantee that if you have a conversation with a hundred customers over a period of a few days or a week, that you would be able to uncover enough information to determine those two measures I alluded to earlier: your "at risk retention rate" and your "customer survivor ratio." What should one do with this knowledge?

One of the most effective ways to utilize customer feedback is by assigning a small team in your business to review the findings. It's not too difficult to code certain verbatim responses into a number of categories to determine if there are specific trends within the data. However, viewing a potential graphic summary of the highlights is no substitute for reading all of the verbatim comments sorted by question. There are so many valuable gold nuggets of information that can be obtained from a small number of customers. Remember that those companies that use their customers' feedback to make changes and strategic plans for growth will surely outgrow their competitors who rely solely on sales receipts and today's profitability numbers.

POWER POINTS WORTH REPEATING

- Welcomers who staff check-out counters are more interested in your state of mind than your method of payment.
- You should think of a welcomer as a magnet that pulls your customer to your establishment instead of to your competitor's.
- Companies should consider that welcomers can be viewed as another insurance policy: customer retention insurance.
- When soliciting customer feedback, be sure to include people that didn't purchase anything. They are just as important as those that did.

10

Engage Today,
Connect for Tomorrow

BY NOW YOU must be thinking that the term "perfect" and
"welcomer" are almost interchangeable in terms of how to
engage with a customer. Simply assign a welcomer to his or
her location or task, and move on to some other managerial
concern. But that's obviously not the case. Let's face it. Everyone
in business can use a bit of advice, even welcomers. They also
may face the problem of missed opportunities. This problem isn't
simply a matter of missing out on a few business transactions
every now and then. It amounts to thousands of opportunities
that a business—regardless of its size or sector—lets slip through
its fingers every minute of every day. Each of those missed
chances means losing out on a potential lifetime customer.

We already know that welcomers are different. Their
specialness makes them "magnets" that keep customers coming
back. They see customers who interact with them as people
first and consumers second. We know that they like to help

people, that they are observant and engaging, and that they are always interested in what's going on around them. You might be thinking, "But you just said that welcomers can use help now and then." You're right.

When you are lucky enough to find a welcomer already in your employ, or find one during the interviewing process, simply giving him or her a few suggestions can dramatically *decrease* your business "at risk retention factor" (the percentage of those survivors in your entire customer base), and significantly *increase* your business and bottom line profitability. Most of these suggestions fall into the category of *the leave-behind*, the last compartment of the tool kit. Instinctively, welcomers, by their very nature of liking to meet new people and being helpful, hardly need any tools from *the greet* and *the assist*. Although welcomers do automatically employ the philosophy of *Engage today, connect for tomorrow*, they may not overtly communicate *connect with* me, *tomorrow*. It's important not to miss any opportunities, and sometimes even welcomers may not directly say such things as, "I would like to personally wait on you the next time you are in our store," or "I work Monday, Wednesday, and Friday evenings from 5:00 to 9:00 p.m., it would be great to see you again," or "Now that I know what your fabric preferences are, if you would like to give me your e-mail

Good to Great

In Jim Collins's book *Good to Great*, Collins talks about how "good is really the enemy of great." What he is suggesting is that, if you only strive to be good, you will never beat your competition over the long run. Why? It's because you'll reach a certain plateau and remain there.

address I can let you know if something comes in that you might be interested in." It's this additional communication that can make even a welcomer go from *Good to Great.*

THERE ARE PLENTY OF YOUNG WELCOMERS

I WAS MEETING a new friend at a restaurant. We had agreed on a time of 8:15 p.m. Since I'm typically an early bird, I arrived fifteen minutes early. However, at our appointed time, my new acquaintance had not arrived. Nor did he arrive by 8:30, or even 8:45. Finally, I called his cell phone. There was no answer, so I left a message. Now consider that during my entire forty-five minutes of waiting, I was standing in the reception area by the hosting-staff stand. If you've ever been stood up, for whatever reason, you know it feels slightly embarrassing, not to mention a bit nerve-racking. However, I was able to observe that the young people on duty by the hosting area were welcomers. All three of them!

They gave everyone who came in a really big "Hello" and smile. They would especially give attention to any small children walking in the door with their parents. I could easily see that they made the kids feel special too. When patrons would finish dining and request their coats, the young hosts would often ask what they had selected for dinner or what dessert they sampled. It wasn't just their interest and interaction that made them special. They helped create an aura of good feeling. Although I got stood up, it turned out to be unintentional. It was simply a result of miscommunications. Even though I was a bit perplexed while I was waiting, I felt comfortable being there, because the staff was understanding, and told me as much. Nonetheless, I would walk over to the hosts and explain that while I wasn't sure what happened to my contact, I'd keep them posted, since the restaurant was completely packed that day. They weren't the least bothered by the fact I was standing in the waiting area.

"Mr. Shapiro, don't worry about it," one of them said. "Whenever your friend does show up, we will take care of you." And, I knew that they would.

Waiting alone had an unintended benefit. I got the opportunity to view the younger generation of service people in action. From my observations that night, as well as experiences on other occasions, I refuse to accept the view that young people don't get it. I have found so many young welcomers in my travels that it has been refreshing.

The following week, when another friend, Robert, was coming to town, I suggested the same place: a business whose staff made me feel comfortable in a somewhat discomforting situation. Our meal was delicious, and the service was excellent. When we arose to retrieve our coats, the two hosts, Emily and Florian, asked us for impressions about our experience. I mentioned that it was not only great, but that it was so special that I wanted them to know it. I also revealed that my friend, Robert Spector, and I were experts in customer service (Robert has written several best-selling books, including *The Nordstrom Way*, and his latest release, *The Mom and Pop Store*). They then asked us to point out our waiter. I did so, but was sure to add that it wasn't simply the waiter that made for a terrific experience, but that they too contributed to our enjoyment by being considerate, attentive hosts. As the hosts, one of their important tasks is to welcome patrons to the restaurant, and of course, since they are usually the first staff members you're likely to encounter as you walk in, they should make a good first impression. In this case, the restaurant (whether the management knew it or not) had the perfect people for the job: welcomers.

"Please come back to our restaurant. We would love to have you as regular customers," they informed us. This is a perfect example of a phrase in *the leave-behind* compartment. You can be sure they left us with a positive and memorable impression. If they hadn't, I wouldn't be writing about them now. In fact, I probably wouldn't even remember them by now.

IS GOOD CUSTOMER SERVICE SIMPLY ENOUGH?

MY COUSIN ERIC told me about a terrific service experience at one of the large homebuilding supply chains. He visited the store branch to purchase bags of water-softener salt. You may know that these sizeable bags are bulky and heavy, not the type of items that you'd want to carry, particularly if you recently had back surgery—which is just the position that Eric found himself in. After finding the items he wanted to purchase in one of those seemingly mile-long aisles, he went in search of a store representative to help. Finding one a few aisles over, he asked the young man whether he'd follow him so as to help place the bags into his cart. The associate said he'd gladly help, and followed Eric back to his cart. However, Eric realized that he'd also need help in transporting the bags from the cashier to his car, so he asked the associate if the store had staff by the check-out counter that would be available to assist.

"Sir, you need not worry about finding someone to cart your items through the parking lot," the salesperson said. "Are there people by the door to assist me?" Eric asked." *I'll* assist you," the young man said. "What I'll do is stand on line with you for as long as it takes, and then carry the stuff out to your car."

He was true to his word. To top it off, when Eric opened his wallet to offer a well-deserved tip, the associate adamantly refused it, and wished Eric a good day.

Now, that is a great customer service story. This scenario could have been converted into an "Engage today, connect for tomorrow" example with just one additional step. Can you figure out what that step could have been? It's very simple. After declining the tip, the associate could have said, "My name is Juan. An important part of my job is to help our customers. I'd look forward to helping you again the next time you need anything that might be available in our store. My hours are 3:00 p.m. to 8:00 p.m. on weekdays. If you don't see me right away, just ask the front desk to page Juan." Now that would have been a perfect "Engage today, connect for tomorrow" transaction. In fact, one could expand it to "...connect for tomorrow and the next day and the day after that." And how long would that additional step have taken? Maybe thirty seconds.

Am I going overboard with this suggestion? Am I unnecessarily criticizing a sales transaction that was really excellent to begin with? Possibly. But remember that I'm discussing how to move from good to great. When a service or sales associate mentions he will personally assist the customer the next time, the shopper will recall that fact, since it means he can look forward to the same high level of assistance the next time, thus alleviating any worry that the next visit might not go as smoothly as the first.

Adding these little "touches" will make the customer feel you were pleased to meet and engage him today. If you do, that extra step of "connecting for tomorrow" will just come about naturally. Why? You're communicating that you'd like to get to know him better as a person—not simply a customer.

I would also like to discuss another extremely important concept that is directly related to the subject of "missed opportunities." It has to do with the topic of wanderers. Who or what are these wanderers? A wanderer is someone who, by chance, walks by your store in the mall and then walks in, or sees your building on a highway and pulls into the parking lot, or finds you on Google and decides to explore your website—all these events setting off a search for a product. One of the literal definitions of a "wanderer" is someone without a home. In many cases a "wanderer" may not have yet found his favorite place to eat, buy clothes, get his dry cleaning done, have a haircut, or what have you.

Simple Steps to Demonstrate "You" Want the Customer Back

- Make sure you communicate to your potential customer that you would like him or her to come back.
- Encourage the person to take you up on the offer; give the individual your name (you could offer to write it on the reverse of the establishment's business card).
- Suggest that the person ask for you specifically when he or she returns.
- Offer to provide your job schedule, so that he or she can time the return visit when you're at work.

Wouldn't it be great for your business if these wanderers ended up calling your business "home," because you made them feel welcomed, important, and appreciated?

I don't understand why companies don't get this. It's not difficult to connect the dots. Just keep in mind that, in so many instances, a business has just one opportunity to make a customer feel important, appreciated, and welcomed. Since the dawn of civilization, people have relied on first impressions to make judgments. Although I can't prove it, I bet that ancient humans, when forming teams to hunt buffalo, decided who would be a worthy partner on the basis of first impressions.

A PHONE WANDERER

I READ ABOUT a new café that opened in our neighborhood. I called the restaurant on the following Monday afternoon, but was greeted with a recording that informed me the eatery wasn't open on Mondays. What message did *I* leave after the beep? Here is the gist of it: "Hello, my name is Richard. I've heard that your restaurant has received some very favorable reviews, so I called to request a reservation for Monday. I hope I can come another time. Here is my telephone number . . . ."

Did I ever hear from the restaurant again? No. Did I ever eat there? No, again. Imagine if the restaurant's owner had called me on Tuesday to say, "Hi, Mr. Shapiro. This is Gerry. You called us yesterday. I'm sorry you were not able to dine with us as we're closed on Mondays, but we would really like to have you visit our restaurant. The food is delicious, the service is special. We would love to meet you so that you and your family enjoy a special meal with us. Is there another day when you might be able to join us?" You don't need to be a rocket scientist to have enough forethought to make that call. It is common sense. Wanderers can be turned into lifetime customers if businesses just think. Don't simply do what you've done in the past, because if you're business isn't doing as well as it could, that's just where you can find the cause.

As part of my research, I have visited dozens and dozens of retail stores throughout the country. Most sales and service people would robotically ask me whether they could be of assistance. My response was, "Just looking." Then, I would try an experiment. I would pause, and then add the following: "Actually, I just moved into the neighborhood and wanted to see what kind of merchandise you had."

I tried out this tactic in a variety of places: shoe, sporting goods, and clothing stores, just to name a few. However, not once did a staff person say anything to engage me, not even something as simple as this: "I'm so glad that you stopped in" or "When did you move to the area?" or "How do you like the neighborhood so far?" or "How did you hear about our store?"

Let's rewind the video in that store's security camera for a moment. Imagine if someone had responded to me as follows: "Glad you came in.

Missed Revenue and Profit Opportunities

Companies are missing major, major, *major* opportunities to turn the initial interactions with wanderers, whether on the phone, online, or face-to-face into customers for life. If a wanderer is lucky enough to communicate with a welcomer, the chances that the wanderer becomes your new family member is increased many times over.

What's your name?" That basic inquiry could open the door for communication that would last well beyond that moment.

Let's hear what a welcomer might specifically say after she found out someone had just moved into the neighborhood: "Well, Rich, my name is Barbara. I'm the manager of the store. We really have wonderful merchandise here. We have stuff that is unique and that you probably will not find anywhere else. And more important, we really value our customers and appreciate their business."

Here are some other things a sales or service associate might include:

- "I would love to know how you like living where you are."
- "How does your family like their new home?"
- "By the way, I'm generally here on the weekends, so please stop in when I'm here so I can take care of you personally."

Yes, engaging today and communicating for tomorrow makes a difference! And that's the way to transform a wanderer (and remember that a wanderer may have come across your business simply by chance) into a customer for life.

TREATING A WANDERER AS A LIFETIME CUSTOMER

I WOULD REALLY like to know if certain establishments ever teach their associates that, when a person walks in to their business, they can look at and treat him in two different ways.

One is the way a welcomer would view the person, as someone who potentially could be a lifetime customer, and the other is to view the person as just one more widget knocking on the door. I just don't understand why so many businesses don't see the wanderer as, not just a potential customer for today, but a lifetime customer for tomorrow.

I'm sure we have all walked into a restaurant and the so-called host or hostess tells you that they're all booked and that's it! It's almost as if they are happy to tell you that they don't need your business.

This attitude isn't simply inappropriate, it's deadly for future business. However, a welcomer knows *exactly* how to address a situation like this, and a recent experience of mine provides a perfect example.

I was meeting two friends for lunch the week before Christmas at a fairly popular restaurant that is known for excellent food and truly good service. Knowing that it was a holiday week, with many folks celebrating the festivities, I made a point of calling in advance to make a reservation. I ended up checking in before my two friends arrived. Now here was a restaurant that understands who should be at the front desk. It was Mr. Shapiro this, and Mr. Shapiro that, and don't worry, Mr. Shapiro. We will keep your table available until your friends arrive. In short, they did everything to make me feel welcomed, and to allay any concern I might have that our table might be allocated to a party that was ready to be seated. In fact, there were several parties of four or more that had arrived without reservations. They were all inquiring about being seated. Just as I had suspected: the restaurant was completely booked. Instead of simply telling the "walk-ins" that they could not be accommodated with a typically curt statement like, "Sorry, we're all booked," the welcomers at the reception station apprised the diners of the situation, and then recommended *another* restaurant close by. The hosts were even more accommodating. They insisted on *calling* the restaurant before the parties left the premises to ensure the restaurant they had suggested had available tables *and* that the guests would be welcomed, and given the same courtesies as guests that had made advance reservations. How often do you hear of a business recommending a competitor and contacting the competitor to make sure they would be congenial? To the average person, it might seem that the effort is not an efficient use of time. But he or she would be wrong. A welcomer knows better. A welcomer treats everyone as a person whether they do business directly or not. In this case, they did not want their customers to go on a wild goose chase only to be literally left out in the cold. They were engaging their customers today . . . and communicating about tomorrow. They were letting their customers know that they were important. If you think such service is unnecessary or excessive, consider how you would like to be treated in such a situation. Where would you consider dining the next time you were out for a holiday dinner? Yes, I thought so!

CANCELLING A RESERVATION

ON ANOTHER OCCASION, I was supposed to go away for the weekend and had made a two- night reservation at a small hotel in upstate New York. When I found out I had a business trip that was going to conflict with my weekend plans, I called the hotel and told them I needed to cancel the reservation. A standard response would be as follows: "Thanks for notifying us. I will cancel your reservation right now. Here is your confirmation number."

Luckily, my call was answered by a welcomer, which meant his response wouldn't be a standard one. This is what he said: "Hi, Mr. Shapiro. This is John. I'm sorry to hear that you are not able to join us, but we would really like you to stay with us on another occasion. When you are able to review your schedule and see what might be another good weekend, please call and ask for me. I'm generally here on the morning shift during the week, and I will make sure that I take good care of you. I know you would love it here." Now that's a perfect example of "Engage today, connect for tomorrow."

So you've invested money and time to bring in new customers. Consider what can happen if one of those potential customers simply calls your business to ask for directions or to inquire about business hours. In many cases, the caller's introduction to your company is via an automated response program that provides impersonal menu options. Worse, if a caller contacts your enterprise *after* business hours (and this is most likely to happen with someone unfamiliar with your company), imagine the frustration of hearing the phone at the other end ring on and on. Or, the prospective shopper will get a curt message like, "Our business is now closed. Please call back during our regular business hours." Another possibility is that the caller will speak to a staff person that happens to work at night (but has no connection to sales or service), who will say something to the effect, "There's nobody here. Call back tomorrow." These two latter possibilities aren't much better than the drone of a distant phone ringing.

The fact that a potential customer visits your business when it *is* open doesn't guarantee that a relationship will develop either. If there is no one there to engage the shopper, there's obviously no possibility for a connection. Will that person visit your store again? Maybe yes, maybe no. That makes as little sense as a manager asking a salesperson, "Did that shopper pay for the item?" and the associate responding with, "Maybe yes, maybe no."

Companies that understand that a key component in their transition from good to great is, in part, having excellent people have a better chance *to become* great. Companies that know the value of welcomers will become more profitable, because they will be able to reduce that nine to twelve percent expenditure budgeted for marketing that is targeted to bring in new customers. They will create a cadre of loyal consumers that will provide you with business and be your company's best advocates for potential

Customer Service: New Rules for a Social Media World

In Peter Shankman's book, *Customer Service: New Rules for a Social Media World*, Peter writes: "In a world where social media is quickly becoming the norm, the same rule is "true." You want to make sure you keep your customers when your company has a breakdown.... You'd better make sure you've spend all your time up until that point building the most solid foundation possible. You want to use current customers to bring in new customers. You want to make the customer so happy that they'll go and do your PR for you, without you even asking (customer-driven PR is the coolest form of PR there is)."

customers. This loyalty will be the major reason a customer doesn't disappear from your radar when a prospective competitor hangs a shingle in the town next door. What may be surprising for many people in business is that the explosion in Internet marketing doesn't alter the equation. Consider one of the prime marketing features of many self-service websites: customer reviews. Who else but loyal, enthusiastic customers are most likely to give you those five-star ratings or those glowing capsule reviews for the entire virtual world to see?

HEY, THERE IS ONE ON EVERY CORNER

I'M OFTEN AMAZED to count just how many gas stations are clustered around the cross sections in many towns. It's common to see four or more of them, each occupying the space at one corner or near the corner where two wide avenues transect. In nearly every state I've driven in, I've noticed how the person behind the counter that's in charge of transactions can make such a difference to the patrons. I can guarantee that if you owned a gas station and positioned a welcomer at the counter, before long your station would be doing more business than any of the three, four, or five others located within a hundred yards of yours. A welcomer would learn people's names (recalling them from your credit or debit card) and greet them by name the next time they walked in. A welcomer would inform them of any special deals or promotions going on at your business, and if you need directions, a welcomer won't just give you a shrug if he can't help you directly. He will find someone that does, or lend you a map to find out for yourself. With a welcomer in contact with your customers, those wanderers will become regulars. They won't check to see if the station down the road is one penny a gallon less than yours. They won't be focusing on the signs. They'll be thinking about chatting with your welcomer for a minute or two.

It doesn't matter what type of business you have, a large percentage of folks that walk through the door don't return. Many that do return come back for convenience, not because there's a welcomer ready to make them feel important, appreciated, and valued. They are just survivors. But when people are made to feel appreciated, they notice even if they don't tell you they do. However, they are making a mental note to themselves. It might be, "Hey that was a good experience," or "The people in that store are really nice," or "I'm shopping *there* again when I'm in the area." What's the evidence? It's in the fact that Mary (whom I mentioned in Chapter 9) had a check-out line that was longer than the others. It's evident because that one store at the mall has been there forever while you've noticed others come and go. It should be clear if there is one store in the shopping center that's more crowded than the others. There's a magnetic force in that store, human magnets in the form of welcomers.

TREATING CUSTOMERS AS CUSTOMERS IS EQUALLY IMPORTANT AS YOUR SERVICE OR PRODUCT

I SAW A YouTube video about a cleaner in the Midwest, whose business had increased over 30 percent during the last year. This was at a time when the average garment cleaning business was down 10 percent. The managers attributed their success to the fact that they had adopted a "green" policy to make sure clothes would be handled in an environmentally safe way. However, a second reason was the way they treated customers. Here's what they do. When their telephone rings, they see the customer's ID information displayed on the LCD screen, so they answer the call with a big, personal "Hello." They ask how the customer is doing before conducting any business. Then, if the customer is a regular, they ask if the customer would like to have her items picked up at the regular time. They have differentiated themselves through this method. They understand the value of providing good customer service, and the equally important element of demonstrating how much they value and appreciate the customer. When a new customer calls, I can guarantee he or she is greeted by a welcomer that is so naturally welcoming that the customer never thinks the store has any "method" at all.

If your company can identify first-time customers or potential customers, and know the importance of that first impression, your rewards can increase exponentially. If you're relying on the fact that your prices are a few cents lower than your competitor's, or, in the case of a gas station, just one cent lower, remember that a competitor can come by and change that variable overnight.

Remember that good customer service is great for today, but making a customer feel welcomed, appreciated, and valued via engagement, will be key to securing repeat business.

POWER POINTS WORTH REPEATING

- Companies are missing major, major, *major* opportunities to turn the initial interaction with wanderers, whether on the phone, online, or face-to-face into customers for life.
- Although welcomers do automatically employ the philosophy of *"Engage today, connect for tomorrow,"* they may not overtly communicate *"Connect with me, tomorrow.*
- Companies understand a key component in their transition from good to great is, in part, having excellent people that have a better chance *to become* great.
- Certain statements such as, "I just moved into the neighborhood," "This the first time I'm in your store," and so forth, should trigger a welcoming response.

11

Finding Authentic Welcomers: Let the Quest Begin

IF YOU ARE either a business owner or a manager of a department or an entire company, I'm going to recommend that you go on a treasure hunt to find those most valuable of sales and service people, the welcomers. The first place we'll look for them is where you work. However, since every reader of this book is also a consumer, we're going to include a hidden treasure map of all the welcomers out there that you meet in your daily life. They could be among the staff at your local supermarket. Perhaps the receptionist at your family dentist's or doctor's office is a welcomer. Think of all those speedsters at the fast-food place or the coffee bar that you stop by on your way to the office. There might be a welcomer among them, maybe even two. So let the quest begin!

I'll help you get started, but by now, you really don't need much assistance at all. I've already provided you with lots of clues regarding how to identify one of those Doctors of First Impressions. Do you recall a front-line service person that made you smile during that first encounter (you may not even have realized it)? If you do, you may have been interacting with a welcomer for quite a while now. Think back. Did the person give you a warm and genuine acknowledgement? Did the person say, "Hello" like he or she meant it? Did this individual automatically engage you in a conversation? Go out of the way to help you? Did this sales or service person notice something you were wearing and tell you how nice it was? Did the person behind the counter say something like, "Hey, the next time you are in the area, stop by and say, 'Hello'?" I could list a dozen more clues, but if you've been reading this book, I think you know them by now.

What about the way a customer service person made you feel? Do you recall one that made you feel comfortable and relaxed? Did you feel that he or she really wanted to know how your day was going so that you answered honestly? If so, did this encourage you to find out more about them? Or maybe you were on the way to his or her place of business, and even before walking through the door, you looked forward to speaking with Agnes, or James, or Fred, or Keisha? I don't need to provide any more clues. If you've been reading this book, you should be able to identify others on your own.

> **Chip Conley, CEO of Joie de Vivre Hospitality**
>
> "The leaders I most admire are those that look at business as enduring and transformational—as opposed to short term and transactional"

If you answered yes to any of the questions I provided, or recalled other welcomer behavior on your own, you have probably found that rare individual, a welcomer.

Robotic behavior is a bit more subtle, but it doesn't take much study beyond welcomer basics to identify it in action. They are the people who have their scripts down pat. While there may be slight variations to the wording, the language they use is more or less interchangeable: "Next in line please," or "Did you find everything you need?" or "Will that be debit or credit?" or "Do you know about our store's discount program?" I'm sure you can think of others. Another telltale sign that you are dealing with a robot is his non-verbal communication. A member of the robot group may recall that you stopped by just one day before, but he doesn't acknowledge that fact. His face doesn't display any signs of recognition. He doesn't display much expression at all. The reason is because most robots see customers as widgets. Ask a robot to describe two or three of their previous ten customers. Most likely she won't remember. Worse, she won't have any idea why she *should* remember. Based on my informal observations, I'd estimate that a welcomer will remember at least five of them, which makes perfect sense. For a welcomer, each new person is just that, a person. He or she is secondarily a customer. It also seems that welcomers have a gift for remembering people. It could be that these two qualities operate hand in hand. I'm thinking now of the waiter, Mohammed. He not only remembered our names, but what we had ordered as well. And we had only dined at his restaurant once before.

As I mentioned in Chapter 1, you will probably never see an interaction with a sales or customer-service associate the same way. Once you've dialed the phone, you will be thinking, "What kind of service provider will I be getting?" On the phone, the respondent's voice quality will most likely reveal to which category the person belongs. When you get a welcomer, it's like heaven. You know that you've reached someone who cares about you and your question. It's in her tone, her mood, and what she says beyond just the facts.

ONE OF MY FAVORITE WAITERS

IRON IS ONE of my favorite waiters at a nearby seafood restaurant. He has an uncanny ability of sensing when I just walk through the door. He shakes my hand and asks me how I am. He tells me he has a table open in his area and will let the manager know that he wants me to sit in his section. He tells me about his past travels and his upcoming vacation. He recounts his recent trip to his sister's house in upstate New York. He explains what he is doing for the holidays. He does this in between serving many tables, which he completes in a timely, friendly manner. Do you recall that I mentioned earlier that welcomers were multi-taskers?

He is a perfect example of a welcomer. In nearly every case, a Doctor of First Impressions can do more than one thing at a time and do them well. When I've finished my meal, Iron lets me know he looks forward to seeing me back. He engages for today and is always communicating for tomorrow. Iron wants to see me again, and I look forward to seeing him too.

MY NEWEST FIND

THEN THERE'S JEFFERSON, one of my newest finds. By my second visit to the local branch of a coffee bar chain, I found out what days he worked, where he was going for his associate's degree, what he was studying, and where he planned to continue his education. He learned about my two sons, Matthew and Michael, and what each did for a living. He learned that I made a "reverse commute" each morning—from my small abode in New York to my business in New Jersey.

Jefferson didn't wear a badge that read, "Jefferson the welcomer," but everything about him signaled that he was one. The next time I visited his shop, Jefferson waved and gave me a big welcoming smile as I walked in. You could say that smile and the warmth are etched in my mind. Why? I didn't coin the term Doctor of First and Lasting Impressions without good reason.

NUT SHOP

EARLY ON IN my research, I walked into a store that specialized in selling nuts and other snacks from all over the world. That's where I found one of my first welcomers. What struck me about her was that she seemed to really love her job. When I mentioned this to her, she told me that she had a passion for customer service. Now, officially her title was "sales associate," but she viewed her main job as helping people. Like other welcomers, I learned that, from childhood, she had a history of helping people.

Also, don't forget those welcomers who write an e-mail that instantly make a connection. Before the world of electronics, people wrote letters and notes to others, in which they communicated warmth and caring. There is no reason why e-mail can't convey the same sentiments.

We also discussed that a large number of robots who haven't previously acted and thought like welcomers may be excellent candidates for Welcomer 101. By employing the tools of *the greet, the assist,* and *the leave-behind,* a robot who wants to be a welcomer-wannabee can achieve his or her new goal, but he needs to really want it. You can't force a robot to act and think like a welcomer. Present him with the concept, and if he acts enthusiastically about his new and exciting role, give him the tools to use. He will appreciate that you, as a business-owner or manager, have given him a new opportunity to view his role in a new manner.

If you've read through this book, you are now qualified to be an official "welcomer appreciator." You need not hand out certificates when you meet welcomers, but you should be vocal about how much you appreciate their service and their interest in you as a consumer and person. Ask the welcomer for the name of his or her supervisor. If the manager is present, speak to him or her. Tell her how valuable her welcomer is. If the supervisor isn't around, get contact information and inform the manager of the fine service you received from the welcomer. Explain how that is precisely the type of service you'd like to experience with *all* service employees. Using this strategy, you're bound to make contact with someone in the organization that has input into customer-service policy. Eventually, the concept of the welcomer can become part of the business vocabulary, and it should be. Business executives will become convinced that such people are invaluable, should be placed in front-line positions, and be rewarded for their special skills. In effect, the welcomer has the honorary degree of Doctor of Customer Service.

LET'S SPREAD THE WORD

I'VE MENTIONED THAT sometimes technology can be a danger to good customer service if it's not consumer friendly. On a visit to a restaurant, instead of a waiter bringing a check, he brought a hand-held terminal where he instructed me to enter the tip amount as he was looking over my shoulder. To me that's where technology and the customer experience don't match up. It made me feel uncomfortable after a very enjoyable meal. What a shame that last impression made. However, I'm hopeful that you will be using technology to spread the *welcomer* word.

I hope that, if you are responsible for hiring sales and service associates, you will be excited to learn that welcomers, and potentially welcomer-wannabees, can make your business stand-out. It can make your business become more profitable and shield you from current and future competitors, who can move in at any time, in the form of brick and mortar or on-line. Since all business owners and managers are consumers too, you can start honing your skills looking for welcomers in your own travels. That will provide you with the added benefit of making you a better "welcomer finder."

You can even play what I'm calling "the welcomer game." Here's how it works. When you enter a new store with several friends or acquaintances, ask everyone to categorize the customer and sales associates. After you leave, see if any of you identified a welcomer. If someone has, share the discovery.

One of my goals in writing this book is to try to improve customer service for all of us. As Tony Hsieh, CEO of Zappos, says, "Zappos is about delivering happiness to the world." In Chip Conley's 2010 TED keynote presentation, he stressed that the worth of a country should not be based on its gross national product, but rather on its gross national happiness.

I'm hoping and expecting that consumers will start to use the terms welcomer, robot, indifferent, and hostile on social media sites when describing their most recent customer experiences. Through tweets, posts, and blogs, having a more consistent way in which to describe a consumer's experience will make it easier for all of us to gain a better perspective on the experiences we might have ourselves. I'm also hoping that, in turn, it will make companies more educated about who they are placing in front-line positions to interact with their most important assets, their customers.

Remember: Good customer service is good for today. Having a welcomer provide good customer service will make you return tomorrow. That's a big difference.

LET'S SHOW CUSTOMERS THAT YOU ARE GLAD THAT THEY CAME

I'M A FAN of some of the old sitcoms, and one of my favorites is *Cheers*, one of NBC's longest-running series, airing from 1982 to 1993. At the beginning of every program were these lyrics from the show's theme song: "Sometimes you want to go where everybody knows your name, and they're always glad you came."

The talents behind this song are Gary Portnoy and Judy Hart Angelo. Gary Portnoy also sang the original rendition. Why can't businesses—large or small, local or international—understand that, while consumers may not expect you to know their name, they do expect you to demonstrate that they're glad you came.

That's what it is all about: making customers feel that they are important, appreciated, and valued, not on their fifth visit, not on their tenth visit, but on the first and every subsequent one. You should also consider that many customers only stop into your store once, happen to call your company just by chance, or find your website by accident. You may never have an opportunity to engage a customer on his second visit, call, or sequence of mouse clicks unless you have the right people to engage him on the first transaction.

When I walk into one my favorite places and they give me that big smile or handshake (sometimes even a hug), it makes me feel so good inside. It makes me feel like people care about me as a person.

Just a few days before I began writing this section, I was out for dinner at "my" Cheers. Instead of receiving the restaurant bill, I got a handwritten not from John, the manager, which read: "Richard, thanks for being such a loyal customer. Your meal is on us. Your friends at Bar 6, Enrique, John, Phoebe, and Lismam."

How do you think that made me feel? I think you know.

ACKNOWLEGMENTS

THE WELCOMER EDGE: *Unlocking the Secrets to Repeat Business*, could not have been written without the help of numerous friends, colleagues, clients, and family members. I would especially like to extend my profound thanks and appreciation to the following people who provided significant contributions to this, my first such endeavor:

- Robert Spector, best-selling author (*The Nordstrom Way, The Mom & Pop Store*), friend, and cousin, for his advice, guidance, and support
- My two loving sons, Matthew and Michael
- The entire team at The Center For Client Retention
- The brilliant folks at my publisher, Vantage Point
- Karen Parziale, 360 Degrees Publicity Shoppe

Additionally, from day one, there were many people who were part of my informal writing advisory board. These special individuals were great at listening, providing meaningful feedback, and encouraging me to move forward every step of the way.

- Jennifer Bassuk
- Jack Covert

- Lisa Marie Dias
- Alan John Gerstle
- Angie Harris
- Brendan Lynch
- Madeline Sagorin
- Sheila Sullivan
- Kristi Weiner
- Sally White
- Julie Wlodinguer

And the HUNDREDS of welcomers I met along the way who really made this book possible!

CPSIA information can be obtained at www.ICGtesting.com
Printed in the USA
LVOW07s0350050915

452967LV00001B/205/P